# In The Belly Of The

## How Twitter Changed My Life In One Year

# Rob Gokee

Fail Whale Press

Fail Whale Press
Published by Fail Whale Press
Fail Whale Press, Long Beach, CA 90802 U.S.A.

Printed by CreateSpace in the United States of America
Cover Design by Allison Vanore
Cover Photography by Raphe Wolfgang/Raphe Wolfgang
Photography
Inside Photos by Shawn Gorritz/3Quarter Moon Photography
Avatar Photos by Raphe Wolfgang/Raphe Wolfgang
Photography

*For Nick and Becca, to show them that you can do anything if you want it badly enough. With or without pants.*

# Acknowledgments

This is the page where I'm supposed to thank all the people that inspired or helped me with the book.

There are none. It was ALL me.

OK, there might be a few.

I want to thank Brian Spaeth, who had multiple conversations with me about his own adventures in writering (which is a word I use based on Brian's use of the word "actoring"), and was there to ask advice of in the beginning. Thanks to Ande Richards, who pushed my when I needed pushing, especially when I was scoring 6 projects at once while trying to write a book, and complained that there weren't enough hours in the day. She didn't care; she just wanted to know when the book would be done. Thanks to my parents, Dawn and Chuck, who gave me everything I needed to be an adult, including the freedom to do whatever I wanted in life, and the perseverance to never give up. Thanks to my children Becca and Nick, who gave my life meaning at a point when there wasn't any. Thanks to Raphe Wolfgang, who is a brilliant photographer and friend, who asked me to his studio in the hills and said "Take off your pants." Thanks to Jorge Urbina who, in the span of 6 months, became a friend who knows me better than some people I've known all my life... even when his hands are in my pants. Thanks to Erin Fleming, who makes me laugh regularly, is the perfect foil, and was instrumental in helping me succeed in the most important gift I've ever bought Allie – a Junior's Cheesecake.

Thanks to Kimberly Prendez, who has always been there when I needed her, and is an amazing friend. She is driven, smart, funny, and she's the first person I called when my life fell apart last year. She listened to me for hours at a time, gave advice, and was there 24/7. She's my best friend, I'm privileged to know her, and I have been and will continue to be there when *she* needs *me* for the rest of her life. Thank you, Kim.

Finally, to Allison Vanore, who transcends beyond the words "Thank You." She designed the cover of this book & edited multiple times, in all her spare time, which is "none." She changed my life without doing anything other than being who she is. Other than my parents, no one in my entire life has had a bigger impact on helping me define who I am. She is the most driven, intelligent, hard-working woman I've ever met, and I felt that way the first time I met her for coffee, before I fell in love with her. She helped me find myself, and I am more "Rob" around her than I've ever been around anyone else. Thank you for your encouragement, support, love, laughter, and for standing by me. I love you with all my heart, and I'm excited to watch your success grow as we grow.

# Table Of Contents

# FOREWORD
## by Brian Spaeth

I strive to not be a walking stereotype.

My path to Twitter was - in contrast to my normal modus operandi - about as stereotypical and generic as it gets. Hear about Twitter, try Twitter, delete account...have friend urge that *you must use Twitter*, try Twitter again...and finally "get it".

The friend who urged me into my second Twitter adventure was none other than the author of this important reading book, Rob Gokee.

Having written several important reading books myself, I chatted with Rob for quite awhile one day about his intentions with this effort. I stressed one thing to him above all others:

*Don't call your shot.*

Seriously, do not announce the thing until you're done with it. You have no idea if you'll finish, nor do you have any clue if it'll come out how you're envisioning right now.

He agreed this sounded like most of my ideas, i.e. pretty amazing and charismatic.

After we got off the phone, I went and got one of my cool dude haircuts I like to get so much, and then noticed the Twitter account for this book was now following me.
"Sigh," I said to myself out loud, admiring my new haircut in the rear-view mirror of my car as I drove

on the freeway and Twittered about doing those same two things while talking on my other phone and changing the radio station.

In any case, the thing about Rob is that he does things his own way. You'll never find one iota of my personal life on Twitter, for example.

While the initial thrust of Twitter's purpose was to tell people "what you're doing", I never want anyone to know what I'm doing, where I am, who I'm dating, what my emotional state is, my favorite state bird, etc. The idea of people knowing these things...just not for me.

Rob...he will tell you all of that and more, and while the announcement of this book and the contents of it are both in complete (and rude) defiance of my entire lifestyle, I have to say Rob pulls it off wonderfully. What is in these pages is touching, real, raw, inspiring, cool, and if you're not the Twitter expert Rob is yet - informative.

Yes, Rob Gokee called his shot and followed that up by nailing it, and I'm glad he did.

In conclusion, I love myself.

Brian Spaeth
January 10, 2010

# Chapter One:
## Welcome. Please Wipe Your Feet at the Door.

Hello. Thanks for buying my book. Now that I have your money, the rest of this bloated monstrosity is going to be made up of volumes 1 through 8 of the encyclopedia (Aardvark through The Plague) and a transcript from an episode of *Who's The Boss* where there's some sort of romantic misunderstanding between Tony and Angela. Enjoy.

You're still here? Dammit, this is going to be harder than I thought. OK, fine. This is a book about me, which is kind of a self-centered topic, and slightly egotistical, but I'd read a book about YOU, so give me a little leeway. My name is Rob and I'm a composer for film & television. I joined Twitter a year ago in an attempt to expand my social network and meet new potential clients. A year later, I came away with far more than I ever thought possible, both personally and professionally. I went through a low I wasn't expecting and a high I didn't see coming, and I chronicled both on Twitter over the course of the year.

That's me.  I'm smiling because you bought the book. Yes, you, (insert your name here).  Thank you.

Although it's somewhat self-indulgent to write a book about yourself, this is as much for you, (insert your name here), as it is for me, because it's a fun way to learn about Twitter if you're not on the bandwagon yet.

How, you ask?  Why, you question?  What, you say impatiently?  Oh.  NOW you're interested in reading the book, huh? (Note to self: change the title of the book to "Crack" and sell it for twice as much).  When I decided to write this book, I had three reasons for doing so.  One, I wanted to share my story with others so that people might take some tidbit of information about the way I marketed myself on Twitter and apply it to their own lives.  Yes, even pantslessness.  Two, I wanted a place to talk about the myriad of things I've gone through and done over the last 12 months (tweeting from the set of a feature film for 11 days, for instance), and maybe make one or two of you laugh.  And Three, I wanted to educate people who aren't familiar with Twitter on how the site works, what the community is like, and how to make the site and it's people work for you, no matter what your business is. For instance, if you collect roadkill off the side of the highway, you might be able to use Twitter to have your "peeps" inform you when there's something dead in your vicinity. Just don't ask me over for dinner. Unless it's a cow. And it's still fresh.

One of the first things you'll notice about this book is the frequent use of the "@" symbol, particularly with someone's name following it. If you're not familiar with Twitter, this is a person's username. Mine is @RobGokee. It used to be @robgokeemusic, but I shortened it recently. If you purchased this book in eFormat, you'll see that every one of those @ names is clickable. I will be calling out individuals by Twitter name throughout the book. If you click on their username, you'll get taken to their Twitter page. My hope is that, after you've read this book, you'll join the site if you're not already there and follow the people I talk about. If I mention them, it's because I talk to them, read their words, and find them interesting in some way. Or, in the case of @aaronkaiser, I find their lack of pants in public interesting. I'm just kidding, @aaronkaiser actually dresses better than I do when I show up at some event I wasn't invited to but decided to crash for the free alcohol. I'm actually the one with the "pants" issue, but we'll get into that later.

If you're reading this fine publication the traditional way (my preferred method), you can still access the Twitter names in the book. Just go to www.twitter.com and add their @ name at the end of the url, like this: www.twitter.com/robgokee. You can do this with anyone's Twitter name in the book. Just follow @cartermason at your own risk. When

I'm done, you'll have your own "search engine" of followers, and you'll already know things about them that are most likely false, but funny. I kid them because I love them all, and they love me back. Some of them love me back in a way I'm not entirely comfortable with, like @axisofphilippe, who repeatedly has "boundary" issues. But I digress.

I've decided the best way to tell my story is to break the book up into 12 months and talk about my Twitter experience during each of them. In Chapter Two, I'll be providing you with a primer that should be helpful if you're new to the world of Twitter (feel free to skip it if you're an "expert" on Twitter, but you risk missing out on jokes. Lots of them.). Chapter Three has some background on who I am and where I came from, so you shouldn't skip that either. In fact, you should read it twice. Every chapter is about my life and the part that Twitter played in it.

My goal is to take some of the mystery out of Twitter so that, if you are so inclined after reading this masterpiece, you can jump right in and start "tweeting." Yes, that's a real word, and no, I'm not drunk at the moment (hides wine glass behind computer).

We shall begin our story in the month of October, 2008. If you get lost.... well, it's not a difficult read, so if you're lost I don't know if I can help you. Just look at the pretty pictures and wonder why the author is so condescending.

Let's get this party started.

# Chapter Two - October 2008:
## My First Tweet

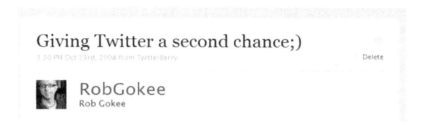

Giving Twitter a second chance;)

3 30 PM Oct 23rd, 2008 from TwitterBerry                    Delete

**RobGokee**
Rob Gokee

There it is, my first tweet. I even "winked," which is kind of lame, actually. In retrospect, I wish I'd said something profound like "I am here to conquer the world" or "Has anyone seen my pants?" In all honesty, this was my second time on Twitter. The first was an attempt to see what the site was about, which resulted in me getting frustrated, not sending a single tweet, and canceling the account after a week. Welcome to my fickleness, brought to you by ADD.

The change in my perception of Twitter came after I read an article in a computer magazine that talked about using Twitter to market your small business. I know what you're thinking. "You read?" to which my reply is "No, I look at the pictures." But I'm always interested in new marketing techniques in my job as a composer, so I forced myself to read what I thought would be a boring article. It was. It was also informative. Go figure. I realized that maybe I should give Twitter another shot before I flamed it all over the internet. Again.

So, I created a new account and started what has now become an obsession for me. At this point in the book, I'm sure some of you are asking "What the hell is Twitter?" Even more of you are asking "What possessed this guy to think he had the skills to write a book? I paid $3,498.12 for this crappy book?!" I will attempt, at this juncture, to start to explain Twitter in a way that's easy to understand.

**What is Twitter?**

Twitter is micro-blogging.

**What is blogging?**

Huh? Do you even own a computer? Most people know what blogs are. They're everywhere, and cover everything. There are blogs about cooking, films, television, books, politics, religion, sex, just about any topic you can think of, someone's created a blog about it. In its basic form it's an online diary that you open up to public opinion. It's a great place to talk about yourself and share your experiences with the rest of the world, and maybe even become famous for it. I've almost always, at various points in my life, kept a journal of some kind. Usually it's full of gibberish, much like this book (rimshot).

There's no rule about the length of your blog, or the content. If you're a cancer survivor who wants to share her/his experience with everyone else, then you can blog about it. If you have a collection of cat hair that you mold into president's faces with gel and

14

hairspray, your audience might be a bit smaller. Take that advice to heart, @purrc4t.

Blogs almost always have a "comment" section. This is where your loyal readers can tell you how exciting and moving your posts are, and how from this point on they'll hang on your every word. Occasionally this is where morons who think they're experts about the topic you blogged about will harass you. Even if it was a blog about your grandmother's goiter, they'll claim to know more than you do, and they usually have nothing better to do than leave comments on your blog spouting off rhetoric like @cartermason at a house party talking about quantum physics.

But more often than not, this is the place where you interact with your readers, many of which have their own blogs. This is the "community" part of blogging, the place where it becomes more interactive than just writing in a journal at home. Some people like this, and others would prefer instead the anonymity of a private journal. Those people are probably not going to like Twitter.

**So what the heck is "micro-blogging"?**

Twitter is like a mini-blog. It's consolidating your thoughts into 140 character snippets and broadcasting them.

It's 2009. Everyone knows what a text message is, and most people know how to send one. A text message is made up of 160 characters. Twitter is a site that takes that format and turns it into a community of "text messages." Twitter gives you 140 characters to say what you want to say, and you can say *anything* you want. This is the "shortened" equivalent of blogging, where you talk about things that matter to you, but in shorter snippets, or "bytes." One thing this does is force you to be more concise in what you say, because you don't have room to be wordy (unless you write a book about Twitter, and then you can prattle on all you want).

Generally the first thing people say when they're presented with an open forum to talk about themselves is, "Who cares about what I'm doing? Do people really want to know what I had for dinner, where I am, or whether or not I'm wearing pants?"

The thing is, they do.

Twitter, in its most basic form, is like a big room where everyone is talking at the same time. You're roaming around the room, listening to snippets of conversations while grabbing crab puffs off the appetizer tray, occasionally stopping to give your two cents about a topic that appeals to you. Sometimes you'll find someone who shares some of the same interests and beliefs that you do, and you'll strike up a friendship. Then later you'll get really drunk, take off your pants, and start grinding on the waiter. Maybe that's just me.

Twitter is a place to talk about the things in your day-to-day life that you feel the need to share. We'll get into more detail later in the book about how that translates into business if you're trying to make money based around marketing on Twitter, but the core of Twitter is that you need to be "human" and interact with people in order for tweeting to work. That's the key to marketing yourself and your business, effectively, on Twitter. But this book is about **me**, not you, so let's get back to talking about **my** lack of pants and what **I** ate for dinner last night (shrimp & fettuccine with asparagus).

## Rob Vs. Twitter

I was aware of Twitter before October of 2008. I'd been using the web-based task program Remember The Milk to keep track of my growing ToDo list, and there was an option to get reminders and send tasks to Milk via a service called "Twitter." In order to do this, I had to sign up for Twitter and then "follow" Remember The Milk so that they could send me direct messages about what I had due and when. It worked... adequately. I am a ToDo list maven. I get excited from a hefty ToDo list.

What doesn't excite me?

Watching @jamiefishback act. Not that Jamie's isn't a good actor, he's quite good actually. For instance, he "acts" like he's my friend, but I know that he's secretly having meetings with @dailyactor about how much they hate me. But I think they drink generic beer and eat fake guacamole dip, so I'm not that jealous.

Anyway, I did not tweet from that first Twitter account. I actually thought the site was confusing and not very beneficial, and it wasn't long before I abandoned it, because I didn't have any patience.

But one day in October that all changed.

I'm a composer. My job is writing music for films, television and webseries, basically all digital media. I went to school for it, and benefited from the education, but to be honest with you, I learned far more on my own. I like to think of college, at least for me, as a place to get my learning habits in order so that I was prepared to study on my own. A

17

lot of the skills you need for being a successful film composer are better learned on the streets than in a classroom. There are other things I learned on the streets, but my mom wouldn't appreciate if I talked about them here.

Although my job requires talent and practice, more than anything else it involves people skills. How you sell yourself, how you get along with other people, how easy you are to work with, all those things have the most influence on whether you're hired or not. Sure, you can't suck at the music writing part either, but you can compensate for not being the "best" guy by being the guy everyone wants to be around.

The best way to influence how you're perceived as a composer is done through marketing. When you're starting out, and even when you're a veteran like Brian Tyler, you need to do your own marketing. In 2009, the majority of this is through social media and the internet. When I started composing on my own in January of 2006, MySpace was rising faster than @brotodeau's manhood in a room full of naked chickens. I spent a lot of time marketing myself on MySpace and garnered lots of new contacts, new work, and money, but by '09 MySpace had started to wane for the independent filmmaker, and I was looking for a new place to whore myself out.

So that fateful day in October 2008, back when I still wore pants, I came across an article about how to use Twitter to market your small business, and I was intrigued. Although, to be fair, it doesn't take a lot to peak my interest. Or lose it. Ask @alliecine, who has to continually juggle things while talking to me to keep me from falling asleep.

The article talked about how Twitter was all about "participating" and "involving" yourself in other people's events and random thoughts. Being the busybody I am, I figured I could worm my way into people's semi-private conversations and maybe get some work at the same time. I'm an ass like that.

On October 23rd, I created my profile and I Tweeted. It was somewhat uneventful. I expected fanfare and fireworks. I was about to quit Twitter again, but then I realized no one was "following" me to read my brilliant update. It was clearly going to be more work than I anticipated.

In order to promote your business effectively on Twitter, you need to integrate yourself into other user's lives, and you need to do it before you sell yourself and your business to them. It's no different than asking the prostitute about her life and family before you get to the rates. The worst thing you can do on Twitter is tweet link after link to promote your business, site or blog, and not interact. People will shun you like you have @TheRealPlague. The only way others will take a vested interest in what you're selling is if they think you care about them as people, and not just another number.

**I Have To Talk To People On Twitter? This Sure Smells A Lot Like Work.**

Take a look at this screenshot from my Twitter profile.

@kevinrieplmusic Look, I already paid you the compliment. Yet there you are, fishing for more. When does it end, Kevin. When. Does. It. End.
*26 minutes ago from TweetDeck in reply to kevinrieplmusic*

@Audnumber That's OK. When it rains in CA I go out in panties and heels too.
*28 minutes ago from TweetDeck in reply to Audnumber*

@PlymouthAgency I know, that's why I was confident throwing your drinking skilz out there.
*28 minutes ago from TweetDeck in reply to PlymouthAgency*

@melissapierce That's why my book is only "partially" business disguised with humor. To trick people into learning something.
*29 minutes ago from TweetDeck in reply to melissapierce*

@Audnumber Why do I get the feeling you still go out in the snow like that?
*30 minutes ago from TweetDeck in reply to Audnumber*

@kevinrieplmusic That's only because I'm procrastinating right now and you're working while tweeting. You're in the book, BTW.
*31 minutes ago from TweetDeck in reply to kevinrieplmusic*

@jiznakefoo Wait a minute. @brksndunngirl is your sister? This is like an episode of Lost.
*32 minutes ago from web in reply to jiznakefoo*

@brksndunngirl Did he used to?
*33 minutes ago from web in reply to brksndunngirl*

When you look at this section of tweets by themselves, they don't make a lot of sense. Some of that is due to my own incoherency and possible drunkenness at the time of tweeting. I blame @alliecine, who puts rum in my coffee. When people first find Twitter, they usually see tweets like these. This is followed by a lot of head-scratching and eye-rolling. Who is this person talking to? What are they talking about? Why did someone give this person an internet connection? He's not going to talk to ME, is he?! It takes time to realize that this is the thing that Twitter is made of.

*Interaction.*

20

If you look at Twitter like a large chat room, except that people wear clothes on Twitter, you'll see that people like to talk about the things that are important to them and their lives. The way "inside" of them, if you're not a serial killer, is to ask them about themselves and comment to them about what they're doing. This includes things that you might think are kind of inane, like what your dog just did or what song is playing on your iPod (right now I'm listening to Brian Tyler's track "Landtrain" from the Fast & Furious score. It's like an orgasm wrapped in a song. But messier.).

Let's go back to the room full of people with crab puffs and alcohol. Everyone introduces themselves and explains to the room what they do for a living, but then the conversation shifts to things that might not be business-related: A kid's soccer game, restaurant recommendations, the game that was on last night, computer problems, who's wearing pants and who isn't, a bad blind date... you get the picture. There's always that one person at the table who's pushy. You know the guy/gal. They keep redirecting the talk to what they're "selling," how great they are, and how the world clearly revolves around them. Consequently, that idiot ends up being frozen out of the bulk of the conversation as soon as everyone realizes what they're up to. At the networking events I go to, that person is almost always @kimberlyprendez. She never shuts up. This is actually funny if you know Kim, because she's the exact opposite. It doesn't matter if he/she is selling the cure for cancer, if you're pushy about it, no one is going to listen.

Twitter is no different. In order to get people interested in your product, whether you're selling books or industrial lube, you have to be interested in the people first. You need to take an active role in their daily lives and, just as importantly, you need to tweet about your daily life. Yes, even the mundane things, like running out of dog food, or being annoyed at having to stand in line at the grocery store to procure said dog food. But there are limitations. For instance, no one cares about the color of your urine. Trust me, I learned that one the hard way. It's important to talk about the things that make up your life. These are the things on Twitter that spark the conversations with new people.

## Fine. So How Do I Know Who To Talk To?

As a business, you need "real people" to buy your product or service. So it makes sense that you should be seeking out "real people" on Twitter to converse with. If you're an actor, for instance, and you're looking to network on Twitter, your best bet is to do a search for "Casting Directors, Directors, or Producers." Doing a search for Producers gives you a lengthy list of people who have the word in their bio and/or tweets. The key thing to do at this juncture is to look at their profiles and what kind of content they're tweeting. You don't want to follow a Twitter account that does nothing but tweet links, or quotes from other people. You want to follow an account that interacts with other users, like this one:

This person, who happens to be a producer, one I'm madly in love with, has a nice mix of conversations with others, and also spends time pushing her own projects. She's having separate conversations with multiple users about things that are (and aren't) related to her business, tweets about her day, and

links to other Twitter accounts that are projects she's working on. This is a smart way to work Twitter. It also takes time. It takes, on average, 3-6 months of conversation to build up a network of followers on Twitter that will not only be interested in what you do, but introduce you to their own followers on Twitter and help you promote yourself. Or, if you want instant followers, you can post a picture of yourself naked as your avatar. It works for @aaronkaiser. Don't go look just to see if I'm lying, trust me.

## How To (Forcibly) Insert Yourself Into Someone's Conversation

By becoming internet "friends" with the people you follow, when it comes time for you to promote a new product, or push a link to a new blog post or an update to a project you're working on, your network of followers on Twitter will retweet the link for you to their followers, who in turn might retweet it to their followers, or follow you because they're new to who you are and trust the person who retweeted you. This is a powerful tool, because you may only have a couple hundred followers, but if you get retweeted by someone who has several thousand followers, your potential base just increased drastically. The reason this book is on the Best Seller's List is because of my followers. Every last one of them. And by the Best Seller's List I mean I hand wrote it in with a purple crayon.

The best way to start the process of making friends on Twitter is to jump in. You'll find that very few people will comment on your tweets first, so you need to start by commenting on theirs. Don't be insulting right away, you need to give them time to figure you out first, then you can talk smack about their pets. Find topics that you have some knowledge of, or an anecdote to share based on someone else's tweet. For instance, "Hey @cartermason, my genital sores look just like yours. Thanks for uploading a picture!" Many times people won't follow you back until you've commented on at least one of their tweets as a safeguard that you're not a spammer or just following everyone blindly. You'll find it's very easy to keep multiple conversations going on Twitter. There's no time limit to replying, you'll find that it sometimes takes people a few hours or a few days to get back to a tweet, it just depends on each user's frequency on the site. Just don't get frustrated if someone doesn't answer back the first or second time you talk to them. Not everyone is as wordy as you are.

## How To Whore Your Business on Twitter. I Mean Sell. S E L L.

There are good and bad ways to promote yourself on Twitter, and things you need to watch when you're speaking for your business. The most obvious way is to provide a brief description and a link to your site:

 **RobGokee**

That's you!

I am clearly the best composerer in the universe, and you should go read my words & hear my music.
http://robgokee.com
less than 20 seconds ago from web

This is an example of someone selling themselves like a cheap whore. And not a good looking whore, one that's clearly been around the block a couple hundred times, if you know what I mean. This moron (I mean, look at that avatar. Really, guy? What were you thinking?) used a brief description followed by a link to their site where you can see what he's offering. This works two ways: First, it pushes your item in a very "non-pushy" way; second, the brevity of the tweet allows room in 140 characters for others to "retweet" it cleanly. Retweeting is when someone likes your tweet enough that they repost it in their own stream. It's a lot like someone borrowing and riding your lawnmower for a few hours, and then showing it off to their friends, too. And by lawnmower I mean "wife." A tweet can only be 140 characters long, and when someone retweets you, you want to make sure there's room for "RT @yourname:" in front of the tweet. It looks like this:

RobGokee RT @robgokee I am clearly the best composerer in the universe, & you should go read my words & hear my music. http://robgokee.com
half a minute ago from web

This shows the followers of the retweeter where the tweet originated from, so they can choose whether or not to follow you if they're interested in your wife. I mean product.

Another example is tweeting a link to a blog post. If your company has its own blog, and you use it to promote events, products or services, you might format your tweet like this:

 **RobGokee**

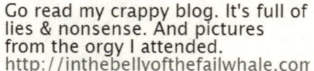

Go read my crappy blog. It's full of lies & nonsense. And pictures from the orgy I attended. http://inthebellyofthefailwhale.com /?p=66
less than 5 seconds ago from web

It's a good idea to have a catchy "tagline" for your blog, something that will entice your Twitter followers to click through the link and read what you have to say. It can be as simple as "A Surprise Waits Ahead!" or as drastic as "I Found a Body...Of Work on Sale in Our Bookstore!" (the second half of the tagline would be on your website). The point is to get them there, and then use your product to keep them there once they've found you.

## So, You're Ready To Become A Whore. Congratulations.

There's an art to when to push your product or service on Twitter. Everyone's stream is different. If you live in the U.S., but your core group of followers is in England, then tweeting a link to your site at 7pm PST when it's 3am in London and your followers are fast asleep or in the middle of having sex is not going to benefit you, unless you're selling something related to what they're doing ("Click here for discount condoms!" might go over well. Then again....). In the beginning of my Twitter experience, I followed some people from London and Australia. It was very odd, at first, to be tweeting "Good Night" as people were tweeting "Good Morning." Be aware of your audience (and your surroundings) when you're tweeting.

## October for Twitter and I

My tweeting in the month of October, since I signed up on the 23rd, was minimal and limited to things like "Working on the score for such-and-such" and "Making the dog for dinner." Actually, my humor had yet to surface on Twitter. That was in November. So let's get over there already, shall we?

28

# Chapter 3 - November 2008:
## It's Time For Some Background

Met the storyboard artist for 11:11, I'm going to start scoring off the animated stroyboards before production begins.

8:35 PM Nov 25th, 2008 from TwitterBerry

Delete

**RobGokee**
Rob Gokee

(I love that I chose a tweet for this chapter that has a typo in it, but that's part of Twitter's charm. When you're typing in the moment it can get messy.)

I was born on a farm in Kansas, an only child found in the crater of a meteorite. At the age of 3, I realized I was different when I lifted a pickup truck off my father, who was stuck underneath it.

Wait, that's not my origin story. That's the guy with the cape. Sorry.

I was born and raised in the suburbs of Los Angeles. I was actually born in downtown L.A., pantsless, and adopted when I was 9 months old. People usually react with the "adoption" comment with "Cool" or

"Wow." I've always just figured that it was the way things were supposed to work out in my universe. My general assumption is that I was actually birthed by a family of crows who, after realizing I wasn't going to fit in the nest, pushed me out on the grass below, where I was dragged by a dachshund to the steps of the adoption facility where my parents paid handsomely for the privilege of taking me home.

I grew up in a middle class neighborhood and had a pretty uneventful childhood. I realize this book might be more interesting if I was kidnapped by a group of farmers and ransomed for a rototiller, but alas, I was just a normal kid in a normal neighborhood. Actually, that's not exactly true. I was a nerdy kid in a normal neighborhood. But instead of spending what will end up being FAR too much time describing my life, I'm going to bullet point 20 things you probably don't know about me. Unless you're @alliecine, then there's a good chance you know most of these.

**One summer I organized the Olympics in my neighborhood.** I actually used cardboard, markers and string to create medals and certificates, and came up with the events. I had about 10 kids participate. Apparently they were bigger losers than I was.

**One of the first musical recordings I ever owned was the soundtrack to The Empire Strikes Back.** On vinyl. When I'd go to school, I'd lie to my friends about who my favorite band was. Mostly so I didn't get my ass kicked. I don't think John Williams would have jumped in and gotten my back in a fight. He was probably busy fending off the guys from AeroSmith beating him with their guitars.

**I love to read.** I used to ride my bike to the library and check out literally a dozen books at a time, and finish them all within the 2 weeks allotted. I remember trying to balance them on my handlebars down the street. How I didn't end up face-down in the mud, books strewn all over the asphalt, I'll never know. In fact, I'll bet if I'd known @brianspaeth back then, he would have thrown a basketball at my head. And then, while I was lying wounded, he'd throw a copy of his book next to my crumpled body on the ground and say "Read this, nerd."

**I have never seen The Godfather.** It's not that I don't want to; it's just never been a priority. If, like me, you haven't seen the film, DO NOT tell people. You will immediately illicit responses like "What?" or "How is that possible?!" and lots of eyebrow raising and mouth gaping will occur. Just pretend you've seen it, and for God's sake don't talk about not seeing it in a book you're writing about a year in your life.

**I was not a fan of high school.** I didn't have a horrible high school experience. I had friends. I had a girlfriend. I lost my virginity. I just never got into being there and "embracing" the whole culture of my school. This is why you will never see me at a reunion for my school. I have no desire to relive those years. I'd rather be in a room full of @cartermason clones, 99 of them, all of them ganging up to get me drunk so they could take pictures of me & their penis' when I pass out. I'm sorry; I meant "peni." I'd wake up with a headache and a tagged picture of me on Facebook, surrounded by 99 peni.

**I loved to write words before I loved to compose music.** I've written most of my life in some form or another. In 9th grade English, Mr. Zant made us write in a journal for the first 15 minutes of class every day. I wrote a 200 page story about my friends and I on the run from the law for a crime we didn't commit, ala A-Team. It's called "The Fugitives," and it sits in a red folder on my bookshelf, all in longhand.

**I'm introverted around people I don't know.** My way around that is humor. I remember the first time I heard Chandler on the show Friends say the line "I use humor as a defense mechanism," I thought 'Wow, that's me.' This makes me a good fit as a composer (the introverted part, not the funny part. Most composers are humorless and boring. @kevinrieplmusic is a good example of this), because you have to be introverted to sit in a room for 14 hours a day writing music by artificial light. Unfortunately, it's not the best personality to schmooze directors and producers at networking events or orgies (If I had a nickel for every "Director Orgy" I've had to go to in order to get hired, I'd have....well, I'd have negative 10 cents. But I'm hopeful that I'll start getting invites soon. I hear @bekemeyer has them all the time). Only recently has the "extroverted" part of my personality come out in spades, but that's a topic for another chapter, specifically June 2009. Hey, come back here, don't skip ahead! I promise there's good stuff between here and there.

**I have an obsession with Bon Jovi.** Not in a "poster on the ceiling" kind of way, in a "Richie and Jon are songwriting Gods" way. I have everything they've ever put out, including some hard-to-find B-sides. It's really the only 80's era band I still listen
32

to and own anything by.  Make fun of them all you want, they know how to write an anthem.  Richie Sambora has had a huge influence on my guitar playing over the years.  Plus, they got all the girls.

**I was married once**, and I have two children that I raised after the divorce.  I don't tweet about them often, mostly because it feels weird to broadcast their goings-on out to the world when they don't have any control over what I say.  I'd be mortified if my parents had done that to me, or even blogged about the horror of raising me, so there's no way I'm going to do that to my kids.  They can handle their own PR on the web.  They're good kids, it's a miracle I haven't warped them by now.

**I am never without music.**  Whether it's in the car, at home or walking somewhere, I will always find a way to put music on.  I need music as a soundtrack to my life, and it's more important to me than any other type of media.  Including books.  You heard me.  Put the torches down, books are nice, too.

**I like boobs.** (looks around) Sorry, wrong book.

**I love television.**  I've been a TV aficionado since I was a small child.  I've never had the same love affair with films.  I watch movies, and there are some that I love unconditionally ("Requiem For A Dream"), but nothing moves me like a good, serialized show.  Television is the medium that brought me into film composing, and the place I'd most like to be.  There's really not any more job security in it than there is in film, you can get canceled at any time.  But there's an art to storytelling a 24 episode story that you don't get in a film, and musically you have the opportunity to expand upon themes, and morph motifs so that they

33

climax as the arc of the show does.... Sorry, I'm getting aroused. Moving on.

**My favorite show is *Buffy the Vampire Slayer.*** No, it's not because I like watching women in schoolgirl outfits. There's a certain stigma attached to a show with a title like that, but let me assure you, boys and girls, that it is so much more a show than you think it is. Joss Whedon, showrunner and creator, took risks with characters and storylines that most shows don't, and he crafted the show in a way that moved me like no other show before or after. I cared about the characters like they were flesh and blood, and the score was amazing and cinematic. In fact, the score for that show is my single, biggest influence in becoming a composer. When I heard Chris Beck's score for *Buffy*, I knew almost instantly that I'd found my career path. That is why Joss Whedon and Christophe Beck are my favorite Director and Composer.

**My favorite film is "Requiem For A Dream."** It's an ugly film. There's no redemption. But it's a beautiful film, with a beautiful score, and the most depressing thing I've ever seen in my life. You'd think that wasn't a ringing endorsement to see the film, but it is. Go buy it now. Seriously.

**This is only number 15?!** My ADD is kicking in; I don't know if I can make it to #20.

**I've never broken a bone**. Except my first finger once when I was messing around in an office chair. I was 25. This is in contrast to the fact that I'm a klutz. I've lost count of the number of wine glasses and plates I've broken over the years. Let's just say a family of 16 in a Third World country could have their own place setting with the amount of dinnerware I've knocked off the counter. At one point in my life, someone I was in a relationship with told me I was being passive-aggressive and breaking stuff on purpose. I contemplated this briefly, but then realized that no, it was my spaziness that was causing the stock at Pier One to rise. Passive-aggressive was when I boiled her Siamese cat. Just kidding. It was a Persian.

**I hate mushy food.** There are very few things I won't eat (insert joke here. Shut up, @cartermason. You've had your turn). Bread-type things that get soggy are the worst. Even pancakes; I need to devour them before the syrup makes them turn to mush. I had Ethiopian food once; the food was amazing, but the spongy-bread that you use as a plate was enough to keep me from going back. I don't know where this weird food quirk comes from, although I'm curious as to why.

**I'm listening to The All-American Rejects right now as I'm working on this portion of the book.** I realize this has nothing to do with my past, but it will by the time you're reading this. I am very open when it comes to music. I'll give anything a shot once. Even country. If I'm drunk first. The first instrument I picked up was the guitar during the 90's, and hair metal was still going strong. I love alt rock as much as I love film score music as much as I love pop as much as I love hip-hop so I'm a cornucopia of musical taste. If I'm drunk first.

**I lost my virginity when I was 17.** Hey, I warned you that this book was going to have sex in it. It was to my first real girlfriend, in the back of a '69 Ford Mustang, which is not the optimal place to lose your virginity when you're six foot three. It was awkward, and about as romantic as @dailyactor, well, just about anytime. But I am a firm believer that whatever doesn't kill you makes you stronger. But not necessarily smarter.

**I don't usually smile in pictures.** It's not because I've got like two teeth, it's more because I always feel fake and awkward smiling on command. My therapist would say that it's some kind of self-esteem issue, and I'd tell her that if that was true, I'd wear two pairs of pants around town instead of zero. Then she'd tell me I was being ridiculous, and that if I wasn't going to take therapy seriously I should just leave. Then I'd apologize and tell her not to worry, I wouldn't embarrass her by putting her in the book.

**Where were we?**

So, it was November. The birds were chirping, the sun was shining, the leaves were turning colors, but I wouldn't know because I'm an introverted composer trying to figure out what the hell this Twitter thing is.

I suppose I should explain what a composer is, since it's my main job, other than "Hack Author." I was dubbed that title by @aaronkaiser. We were at a networking event one day where I stood up and talked about how I was writing a book about Twitter. Aaron said aloud, "That's real? I thought you were joking!" True story. Also, @aaronkaiser doesn't like the word "Holiday" used in place of the word "Christmas." For the record, I don't either. But I like picking on Aaron, so guess who's using the word "Holiday" all over his Twitter page right now? (points at self smugly)

# How I Became A Composer & What I Do

A composer is someone who writes music. I attempt to do that for films, television shows, and webseries. I'm pretty damn good at it, actually. I've always had a penchant for film scores. When I was 16, I started playing guitar, and wanted to be the next Joe Satriani. I realized quickly that I did not have Joe's fingers, but that did not stop me from practicing my ass off. I learned how to play guitar by ear, which is the opposite of learning by reading music. I listened and fumbled around the fretboard until I found the right notes, and then memorized where to go and how to get there in order to play songs. After a few years, you find that your fingers just "know" where to go. It sounds odd, and it's hard to explain in words. I continued to learn this way until college when I took lessons in theory and composition, and learned how to read music. It was there that I gained an appreciation for the other side of music, which is the "learned" method. There's no wrong way to learn an instrument; I don't care what anyone tells you. Just learn as much as you can, and as many methods and techniques as your brain will hold. Mine is full.

Writing music for films is a different animal than, say, writing songs in a band. You're not really writing a self-contained piece of music, you're writing something that's "married" to some form of video. It's an interesting process, and every composer has a slightly different way of doing it. My process for writing has always been to loop a section of video on the monitor and start writing over it. Usually nothing works for the first few hours; sometimes I have to walk away and go do something else, and then when I come back something I originally hated will suddenly sound OK. Then I start

37

shaping the genesis of an idea into something larger, and start filling it out. That's my favorite part of the process, the details. I'll usually get ideas from the script; I'll hear music in my head while I'm reading, but it's that video process that gets things going.

Usually, I sit down with the director and/or producer(s) and talk about their vision for the film musically. Sometimes they're very specific, and sometimes they just hand over the keys and let me run with it. I prefer having direction; it saves time when you start going back-and-forth, tweaking the music here and there to fit what everyone wants.

I'll take my notes, which will also include "where" in the film they want music and don't, and go back to my studio to write. Then we meet again for a "show-and-tell," where I play them what I've got and take more notes. Then I go back and write, and the process continues that way until we're "locked."

Sometimes I get eight weeks to score something. Sometimes it's eight days. It really depends on the film and how much time they have left at the end of post production when it gets in my hands. I prefer less time than too much, which feeds into my procrastination. Once in awhile, I'll get the film and the director will say "No rush, take your time and let me know when you're done." This drives me nuts, because I need deadlines to get things done in a timely fashion. If I don't get one, I'll create one myself and schedule the show-and-tell myself so I can work backwards from the due date.

95% of what I write is on the keyboard, which is actually called a "MIDI Controller." I have some insanely expensive, top-of-the-line samples that get "triggered" with the controller; so that I can play instruments I don't have access to, like 11 violinists at once. Everything gets recorded just like a band would do; all the instruments are written separately and then mixed together. The recording, mixing and orchestrating actually takes more time than the initial writing.

Orchestrating is where you take a melody and harmonize all the other instruments around it. If you write the melody with a violin, then you accompany it with the viola, cello, double bass, woodwinds, brass, etc, so that they fill out the other notes in the key. It's my favorite part of the job, because you get to hear something that sounds "small" become "full" and "whole."

**Twitter in November**

Because I joined Twitter at the end of October, November of 2008 was still part of the "feeling out" process. I had started to accumulate friends. How, you ask? Twitter as a site is the definition of "user-generated content." Twitter users are a lot like snowflakes: No two of them are exactly alike in their approach to the site. Everyone has a different "audience" on Twitter, and there are effective ways to find users so that you're able to maximize your presence and time on the site.

**How To Find Who You're Looking For**

When you look for users on Twitter, especially when you're starting out on the site and need some followers (or in my case, real friends), your goal is to find people who would be interested in the same things you are, or what you're selling. If you're a home builder, it's not going to generate a lot of business by following "cat lovers." In fact, this search will bring up the irascible @ginayates, whose love for her cats is matched by her love of some astronaut named "Scott." Gina is well on her way to having 14 cats, which puts her in direct competition with @betenich, who would rescue road kill if @jfuzell would let her.

The basics of searching for users on Twitter comes down to keywords. For instance, if you're a composer for film and television looking to network on Twitter for business, following "mommy bloggers" is not going to be beneficial (unless you're looking to date mommy bloggers, then by all means go ahead and search. Some of them are pretty funny. But don't call them MILF's. They don't like that, and they might band against you on Twitter and accuse you of being a pig. I wouldn't know, I'm just sayin').

The keywords, as an example, that are going to provide me with the best network might be "Director, Producer, Webseries, Editor, Television, Film, Post Production & Entertainment Industry." If you find @brownambassador this way, you must have typed "Sleazy Director" by mistake. Feel free to start over. These will pull up Twitter profiles that have those words in their profile bio or in recent tweets themselves. Then it's as simple as "Following" them and striking up a conversation about what they're working on and what their future needs are, and finding a way to fit yourself into their equation.

**Where To Search**

There are many sites set up to help you search for Twitter users, all of them slightly different in their own way. One of the most effective search sites is Twellow (http://twellow.com). Twellow has been around for years, and was a popular search engine when Twitter's own was down for revamping last year.  Twellow is great.  For example, typing in the word "Director" immediately yields over 32,000 results.  Typing in the word "Blowhard" will take you right to @jasonburns' page.  @jasonburns is that guy at the party that everyone thinks is funny, and you're secretly jealous of him because he's funnier than you.  But that's OK, because your way around that is to write a book that's funny, so that people will think you're funnier than he is.  Except that he's on the radio, and heard all over the nation. Dammit.

SO, I embarked on a Twellow search for Directors and Producers that were tweeting.  And I found a slew of them.  I also started to tell people in the real world about Twitter.  This was a lot like talking about building a car when all you have is half an engine in the garage.  But I felt like I was starting to "get it," and I was excited to tweet about scoring a feature film, "11:11," that had been in the works for years.  I had signed on to compose the score before the script was even done, so I was not only invited to the casting session and the table read, but on the set itself to observe the process.  The point was to see if I could catch some inspiration and take it back with me, and I was going to tweet about the entire process.

I ended the month of November by following a couple hundred people.  A few of them followed me back, but most of them were waiting for me to strike up a conversation.  Apparently no one told them I was the best thing since wet milk and that they should just follow me instantly.

At the point when I joined Twitter in October, I was 4 years into a relationship with someone I'd met while still in school, and we lived together in LA.  I

41

was happy and things were good.  At least I thought they were good.  We talked, we hung out, we shared dogs and furniture and a life.

Twitter came along at a point when I was in a lull with scoring.  It wasn't that I didn't have work, I had a huge film (11:11) looming over me, and I was reluctant to look for projects that were going to conflict with the scoring of that monstrosity, so I was lying low and taking care of other things on my never ending ToDo List.  My ToDo List is so large and prominent, in fact, that it gets capitalized like it's a proper name.

I saw my advent into Twitter as a rebuilding of my marketing strategy, because it was a different approach than anything I'd tried in the past.  It was also a catalyst that I wasn't aware of; I didn't see then how it was going to affect my life later.  After all, it's just a website, right?

No, it's really not.

# Chapter Four: December 2008
## Loosening My Pants & Wetting My Feet

It appears the reading I'm supposed to be doing has been hijacked by tweeting. (Shakes fist in the air) TWITTER!!!

4:34 PM Dec 23rd, 2008 from web                    Delete

**RobGokee**
Rob Gokee

December in California is more like summer in Colorado. There's not even rain in December. It's the perfect place for me; you can go pantsless like 350 days a year. It makes it harder to market me, ask @PlymouthAgency. She's not getting paid nearly enough money to have to deal with my shenanigans.

December was a slow month. I wasn't scoring anything, I wasn't looking for new work (film production generally is a ghost town from Thanksgiving to January 5th, if a project isn't already underway it's not going to happen) but things were fine at home. Which reminds me...

...I suppose that some relationship background is in order.

**What It's Like To Be In A Relationship With Me**

**I got married right out of high school**. In hindsight it was not the best decision in the world, for very obvious reasons. It worked for my parents, who have been together for like 200 years and still hold hands in public. Gross. But I got two amazing kids out of the deal, so I would go through it all over again just for that. Although I would have married @jamiefishback instead, and I could have carried the kids in MY uterus.

**I didn't have a girlfriend or kiss a girl for the first time until I was 15.** And by 15 I mean 16. It's not that I wasn't interested, I was just insanely awkward. Awkward like @aaronkaiser at a "Holiday Carol" festival with a T-Shirt that says "Take the Christ Out of Christmas & I'll Kick the Crap Out Of You." That was also the year I first had sex. We covered that train wreck earlier. Don't worry; I'm much better at it now.

**I have a problem with people who cheat**, in that I think castration is the best solution. Or spackle. I'm not going to badmouth anyone specifically in this book; it's not really fair when other people aren't able to defend themselves. Especially when there's cheating involved, and not by the person writing this book. But I will say that it took a lot for me to trust again after my marriage ended. I finally realized that the only way I was going to fall completely and hopelessly in love with someone was to give someone 100% trust right out of the starting gate, and take the chance of getting hurt. It's a good way to live, in my opinion, because every person is
44

different, and you can't "categorize" a gender by the actions of one. Trust me when I say I know what the pain of being cheated on feels like, and I'd be happy if I never went through that again. But love is worth the risk.

**I can count the number of people I've dated my whole life on both hands.** I've never dated around, if I'm going to date someone I've got to be able to see that there's potential for it to go the distance. If I don't, then I'm out. It's the only way I can give all of me to someone, and I don't want to open up like that if I suspect I'm going to get hurt.

My current relationship was 4 years long at this point. We got along really well, she was my best friend, and there was no sign that anything was wrong. We met when I was in college, and we worked together, finally moving back to California together in January of 2005. There was nothing that ever made me think it wasn't going to work, and it had been working for a long time. At the point when things fell apart, it came on suddenly and without provocation. Little did I know that introducing her to Twitter would be instrumental in our undoing.

Meanwhile, back in December...

I was invited to the casting session for "11:11" this month, and I was excited. The composer almost never gets invited to anything related to the pre-production process, or even production, and for this film I got to do both. I showed up ready to tweet. We were casting for the role of a drug-addicted young woman who's begging for drugs. I got to sit on the casting couch with the producers. Director Rocky Costanzo decided that I would be the line of sight for the actresses, which I thought was cool.

45

Until they started auditioning.

Woman after woman stared at me, begging for a fix, screaming at me to give them drugs. And I couldn't turn away, because I didn't want to throw them off during their audition. It was emotionally draining. If I had found some crack in my pocket at that moment, I would have thrown it at them. Don't invite me to an intervention, I'll be the guy trying to score more drugs in the parking lot for the person being intervened, except that I don't know how to buy drugs, so I'd undoubtedly screw it up and get arrested and thrown in jail next to @wzzy, who was arrested for stealing rain boots from a small child outside the elementary school. Three times.

During the audition process, I was tweeting. I was also being ridiculed for tweeting, because this was the first time any of the producers had heard of Twitter. They were definitely social media deficient. I gave them a Twitter primer, although I was still new myself, and they seem less judgmental and more understanding. Yes, they still made fun of me.

## You Can Tweet From Your Phone?

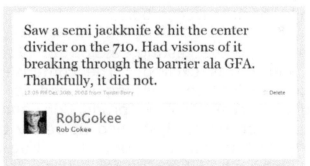

Saw a semi jackknife & hit the center divider on the 710. Had visions of it breaking through the barrier ala GFA. Thankfully, it did not.

RobGokee
Rob Cokee

This is a great opportunity to talk briefly about tweeting by phone. When you're busy, whether you're an actor (@JonathanNail), a Producer (@alliecine) or dress up like a clown and sell sex toys from a dilapidated ice cream truck to housewives (@brianspaeth), you can't (in most cases) sit by the computer all day long, tweeting or checking your Twitter page for replies and messages. Fortunately, Twitter has some nifty mobile applications designed to let you tweet on the go. This goes a long way in showing your followers what we talked about earlier: your "human" side. If you're waiting in line at the post office and a dog runs through the lobby, tweeting about it will elicit responses in a way that tweeting about work won't. Unless said dog is running loose at your office. If people think you're genuine, and like you, then they're more likely to respond to you positively and in turn look at who you are and what you do with more detail and interest. If, for you, this means tweeting from the bathroom, please don't tell the rest of us. I keep trying to explain this to @iamboney, but he doesn't seem to get it. Once you're on Twitter, there's a section for setting up your mobile phone in the "Settings" area (you can tweet by texting). If you've got a smart phone, there are lots of applications that will let you tweet from your phone, check out the "Downloads" section on Twitter's website. My favorite? UberTwitter for the Blackberry. It's an amazing application that integrates itself into your Blackberry OS beautifully.

SO, I was being made fun of for tweeting. Mind you, this was before Oprah decided to devote a show to Twitter and crashed the server, so there were fewer users than there are now, and less publicity. Rocky and Roy, the "11:11" production team, were giving me a rash of shit, and making me feel very geek-like, which is fine because I am a geek. The next day, Rocky called me. He wanted to know if I'd tweet from the set as the official Twitterer for the film. I accepted, despite the fact that it paid no more than I was already getting to compose the score, which was 3 chickens, a cardboard box (flattened) and 16 sunflower seeds, ranch-flavored. I had to negotiate for the seeds. Suckers.

I ended 2008 more Twitter-savvy than I was going in, by about 1000%. And the best was yet to come in 2009.

And the worst. Keep reading, you'll see.

Except you, @lisamurray. You've read far enough, I think you should be writing more of your own stuff instead of wasting all this time reading about stuff you read about the first time around, because you've been following me a long time.

# Chapter 5: January 2009
## Professional & Business Lullaby

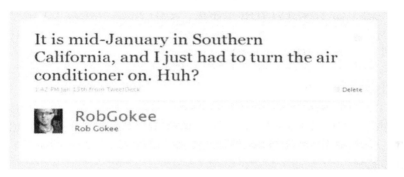

It is mid-January in Southern California, and I just had to turn the air conditioner on. Huh?

1:42 PM Jan 15th from TweetDeck                                    Delete

**RobGokee**
Rob Gokee

I started off the year by canceling my Facebook account. It was a decision based around the fact that a lot of people I was "friends" with had no clue about who I was. It was a political decision, in that it was based around politics. Politics is an easily confrontational subject, much like religion. The issue of gay rights had come up on Facebook, which is a mash-up of both politics AND religion, and when you talk about both at once it's like mixing bleach and ammonia. I'm not gay. But having been married, I think everyone has a right to take that step. Certain people on Facebook wanted to argue the religious aspect of marriage, which I feel is separate.

If I think I'm right about something and it's a topic I have strong feelings about, I'm like a dog in a tug-of-war.  I won't back down until we reach a point when I'll refuse to back down.  It's at this point in the "conversation" that I become an asshole.

I was assholing myself all over Facebook.

So, after a few non-stop frustrating days, I canceled the account.  It was freeing.  At the time, I hadn't really looked at the marketing aspects of the site, and when I did at a later point I created a new account.  My Facebook account is like the PG-13 version of my Twitter page.  I'm less likely to use the word "penis" on Facebook.  Feel free to look me up and friend request me.

I also introduced the girlfriend to Twitter, who took to it quickly.  Her approach to Twitter was more social than business; she was there to meet people. There's some irony there; you'll get it later in the book.

**Desktopping Your Twitter (Yes, Another Lesson)**

Also, this month I started tweeting from a desktop application instead of from the Twitter website.  Once you've become accustomed to Twitter's interface and have the basics down, it might be a good time to look at third-party applications for using the site.  There are plenty to choose from and each one has intricacies that the others don't; it comes down to a matter of preference and what works best for managing your account(s) on Twitter.  Most of the applications offer multiple account management, so you can tweet and monitor more than one Twitter account at a time.  If you're a filmmaker, for instance, you might have separate accounts for each project you're promoting (if you're @alliecine, you're managing like 12 Twitter accounts for each project she's spearheading. You think I'm exaggerating. I'm not), and using a third party application can be advantageous and time-saving. I use TweetDeck. Not only does TweetDeck integrate with Twitter, it also lets you update your Facebook, LinkedIn and MySpace profiles, and you can see all of them in your stream. You can create custom searches and save them to columns (there's no limit), and there's a convenient scroll-bar at the bottom to move from side-to-side. Each of your accounts can have separate columns as well, so that you can track your followers more accurately. One unique feature that TweetDeck has is the option to crosspost your tweets to multiple accounts all at once. The application keeps you signed in to all your accounts simultaneously, and keeps track of them at the top of the screen. You can click on more than one (in the screenshot below, you can see two different accounts highlighted) at a time, and send one tweet from both accounts, which is a huge timesaver.

TweetDeck is free, and works on both Windows and Mac (there's also an iPhone app).

Back to January.

I was starting, very slowly, to accumulate Twitter followers. I had long conversations with @dr0id, whose love for all things PC made me want to be his BFF, and @kevinrieplmusic, who never shuts up. But I wasn't finding any work yet, which was frustrating. It had been three months of tweeting, and nothing had come out of it in terms of business. But I was enjoying it, so I decided to stick with it.

At the end of the month I went on a location scout for "11:11." The locations had already been set, but the director and cinematographer needed to see how the shots were going to be set up at each of them, and I got to tag along.

Unfortunately, I had to wear pants.

We took two vans; I tweeted away, and got responses from some of my followers, which made me feel like I was doing the right thing by sticking with it.

We hit up around seven or eight locations; I tried to draw a little inspiration for the score from the Huntington Beach locale. It worked in a few places, the beach being one of them. I love being inspired musically by things around me. As a film composer, I really need to see the footage from the film before I can get a hard grip on the score. But sometimes, with the right location or moment, I can get snippets of music that will later work in the score.

And that excites me more than sex.

NOTE: This is not actually true.

But overall, January was a slow month, in that I really didn't have a whole lot going on. Also, I noticed that there was a slight difference in my relationship with the girlfriend, in that she was a little withdrawn, and no amount of talking or asking helped me figure out what was "off." That's the appropriate word for what was going on, things were "off." We were still hanging out, talking and getting along, but deep, deep inside my brain I knew something wasn't right.

And I was right.

# Chapter 6: February 2009
## Is That A Bus Bearing Down On Me?

Darriens cigarette wouldn't light on the first take.

11:40 AM Feb 21st from TwitterBerry

 RobGokee
Rob Gokee

As you can see from the tweet above, production started on "11:11" this month, my first time on a film set. Being on a film set is a lot like being in @aaronkaiser's bed for the first time. Initially, you're scared and nervous, and afraid you're going to touch something you're not supposed to, but after a few hours you realize there's a lot of prep for just a little bit of payoff. Weekend One took place at a house in Huntington Beach (Saturday) and a middle school about a mile from the same house (Sunday).

As the composer, and official tweeter, I had pretty unfettered access to the set. I got to stand behind the director and the DP during the shots, and hung out with the actors between takes. I never realized how much prep and setup goes into shooting just one scene. The first scene was the lead (Darian, whose name I spelled wrong in that tweet up there) walking out of his front door and away from the house. It was overcast, so they had to set up lights to mimic the sunlight, and then use huge reflectors to "bounce" the light back to where it needed to be. The camera had to be set up in the right spot and marked. The sound crew had to mic the actors and check the sound levels. Then the actors had to rehearse multiple times before we even got to the first take. It took hours. I began to realize this was normal, and I was in for a long shoot.

Not having a specific job on a film set is a lot like hanging out with @Kevin Stahl. At first it seems fun, and the food is good, but then you're so bored you want to gouge your eyes out with a spoon and feign a stroke so you can get the hell out of there. Fortunately, I had tweeting.

In the morning, people on Twitter were asking me questions and responding to my informative, but somewhat bland, tweets. But by the afternoon, interest had waned at both ends. It was a 14 hour day at day's end, and it felt like it. But I came away with a wealth of knowledge and I was still anxious to show up the next morning for Day 2.

I could not ask for better weather to work to. Keep that rain coming!

2:58 PM Feb 5th from TweetDeck                     Delete

RobGokee
Rob Gokee

The second day it threatened rain. Despite that tweet above, rain is not conducive to a good film shoot when you're shooting outside. We started off on the field of a junior high school, and moved to the front steps of a gymnasium. I was a little more savvy on Day Two, and the behind-the-scenes videographer was late, so I was handed a camera (the same camera used to shoot the film "Amhurst," which I scored the year before for the same production company) and told to shoot stuff. Which made it harder to tweet, but not impossible. Also, it's the first time I shot with anything other than a still camera, so it was an interesting experience. The damn thing was heavy, and you had to move slowly, which is not something I know how to do.

See the Blackberry in my hand? I was tweeting. See that vacant expression on my face? This was a 16 hour day, and this picture was taken by Shawn (3QuarterMoon Photography) at the tail end. I was not the only one who looked like this. We were inside a gym shooting a basketball scene with a lot of kids as extras. The kids were great. The mothers of the kids were a species unlike any other. I've never been exposed to "set moms" before; it was like a pack of hyenas waiting for a giraffe to slow down. And the giraffe was everyone else's kid. It was a "my kid is better than your kid" contest, but played in a passive-aggressive way that came off like they were all rooting for each other, except they SO weren't. There was one "set dad" there, who hung in the circle for awhile until he finally left the pack and went over to the back of his car, fiddling with his phone. I think they smelled his fear and he didn't want to end up as lunch.

At home, things were... fine. There was still this weird air of "offness" that I couldn't put my finger on, but it didn't seem any worse than it was the month before. The girlfriend was meeting lots of new people on Twitter, some of them mutual friends. Some of them were new friends. Again, we spent a lot of time together, talked a lot, we were still affectionate, it's not like there was some wedge between us.

Well, there was. But it was invisible.

Back when I was married, in the months preceding the end of the marriage, looking back, I could see it coming a long time before it did. I didn't want to see it at the time; it's very easy to be in denial when you don't want to "rock the boat." It's kind of strange the way your brain will find justification for the most ridiculous situations or explanations. It's like the logical side of yourself shuts off, or puts blinders up, and instead tells you what you want to hear in order to keep you from realizing that things are horribly wrong. I'm sure it's the same part of your brain that triggers the "Denial" stage of grief when someone dies.

I look at every situation you're put in during the course of your life as both a learning lesson and a building block. There are things that have happened that I wish to never go through again, and were incredibly painful. But those things made me who I am today, and I wouldn't be where I am without them, so they're necessary steps to moving forward. If I can take something from a horrible situation and apply it to the rest of my life in some way, then in a strange way it's worth it. When you keep getting into the same horrible situation over and over again, it's because you're not learning the thing you're supposed to be learning, and applying it.

This was not that kind of situation. There were no warning signs that things were wrong, nothing that needed "fixing," so it was perplexing to say the least that I still felt like things were not moving forward and in some sort of weird "loop." If you look at the relationship like a graph, the months of December, January and February were a flatline instead of an increase.

In my mind.

In hers, unbeknownst to me, it was more of an alarming drop.

March 4th was the day the market crashed.

# Chapter 7: March 2009
## The End As I Knew It

> I think the rain & my site being down
> (until GoDaddy finds a fix) go with the
> theme of the rest of today's events.
>
> 10:44 AM Mar 4th from web                    Delete

 RobGokee
Rob Gokee

You know that scene in any disaster movie where one person knows something really, really bad is coming, and no one else believes him? In my life, that guy wasn't there. Instead, I was the guy in the rowboat facing the other way when the tsunami roared in from behind, wondering why everyone was leaving the beach. That tweet above was typed literally an hour after I realized my relationship was over.

Ahh, March of 2009. I remember it like it was six months ago. (looks at calendar) Oh, it was. March was the catalyst for everything that's followed it, most of it positive. The life I'm living now is 180 degrees from where I was then, and it seems very distant in a lot of ways when I look back. It was a rebirth of epic proportions. But at the time, it was not a happy month.

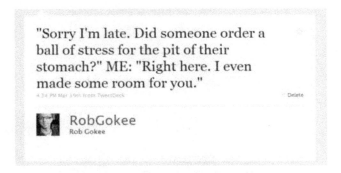

"Sorry I'm late. Did someone order a ball of stress for the pit of their stomach?" ME: "Right here. I even made some room for you."

4:34 PM Mar 15th from TweetDeck                    Delete

**RobGokee**
Rob Gokee

I think this is a good point for a disclaimer. This book is not just about me, it's about the people on Twitter that affect my life. Although I talk about them a lot on here, I'm still attempting to give them some anonymity, which is not an easy thing to do in an autobiographical account of a year in my life, a particularly tumultuous year. I want to preface this chapter by saying that I am not placing sole blame on any one person over the end of my relationship. There are always two sides. My purpose here is to tell you what was going through my head and my actions during this time in my life.

I woke up the morning of March 4th thinking it was a day like any other day. I jumped on Twitter, checked my email, and drank coffee.

Then I found out that my girlfriend was leaving.

It's like when @the beth promises to bake you a cake just for the hell of it, and then comes over with a plate full of crumbs, and frosting all over her mouth going "Cake? What cake?" Relationships end for lots of reasons, and in many different ways. One thing that's almost always the same is that there are signs that things are wrong, things that you might ignore or overlook for a long time until it's too late.

I started the day by checking tweets, and saw one from someone that the girlfriend had been talking to quite a bit. She had booked a trip out of state a few weeks prior, just to "get away," and I suddenly wondered if there was any connection. It was like this weird "sixth sense" that the something that wasn't right was really, really bad. I glanced to see where he lived.

It was the same state she was visiting.

And the same city.

I pulled up the cell phone bill. There were calls on the cell phone bill to an area code in that city. Then I saw that the calls were frequent, for hours at a time, and the last one had been from midnight to 4am, just 2 ½ hours before I got up. I was starting to feel sick.

There was one other place to check: email. That's when I found out that she was leaving. Her friends knew, her family knew, the guy on Twitter CLEARLY knew. I was literally the last one to know. My stomach dropped; I can remember the feeling just by typing it.

The end of my relationship came with very little warning. I knew something was "off," but I couldn't put my finger on it. Never in a million years did I think it was as cancerous as it was. I remember the second I realized it was all crashing down, I could feel my entire insides drop into my stomach, like a fall on a rollercoaster, but slower. I was sitting in the exact spot I'm writing this sentence, on this computer, that morning at around 8am, trying to process the information. 4 ½ years is a long time to be with someone, and the band-aid was pulled off in one yank. I remember it rained all day, and I'm pretty sure I didn't leave the house.

I woke her up and told her I knew. I wasn't angry, I was feeling like the bottom dropped out of my life and I wanted desperately to fix it. She said very plainly that she wasn't in love anymore.

The end of a relationship is like going through the death of someone. A therapist I went to about a week later, who sucked so bad I'd put his name in here if I could remember it, once told me that, in order to move on from a relationship, you needed to picture the other person being buried at their funeral. This image actually made me cry in the therapist's office, but it also made me want to punch him in his stupid face. Instead I dumped him for a better one. But he had a point. You go through the seven stages of grief when you get dumped. For me, the first four happened in March, and the last three (which have to do with moving on) happened at the tail end of April.

**Shock and Denial**  I remember distinctly that I couldn't believe it was happening. I thought, "Wow, universe. This is a doozy of a dream, good job freaking me out, but I'm ready to wake up now. Let's go. NOW. Seriously. This isn't cool anymore." I felt very detached from what was happening, and it was very dream-like for the first few hours. I couldn't process what was happening, I wanted to go back to sleep and pretend that the day hadn't started yet.

64

**Pain and Guilt** Oh. My. God. It hurt. Not so much with the guilt, because there wasn't anything to feel guilty for, but there was regret. I wanted to build a time machine and go back so I could fix whatever the fuck it was that caused things to get where they were. I'd been through it before, so I knew what the pain of your heart breaking feels like. It was almost familiar, like a bully who stopped picking on you for awhile, and suddenly resurfaces. Yes, I'm talking about you, @migroddy. Miguel used to take my pants every day after school and throw them on the roof. The janitor always got them down, but then he watched me put them back on with a creepy smile. That janitor was @robmader. Actually, @robmader and @migroddy are amazing musicians I met on Twitter, and never bullied or violated me.

Until I was an adult.

**Anger and Bargaining**   There wasn't anger until much later, and it was directed more at myself than her and the person she was involved with. I was, however, all about the bargaining. I spent a week trying to coerce her back, trying to fix whatever it was that caused the rift. The problem was, it wasn't something I could fix, because it had very little to do with me. Ultimately, it was about her attempting to fix herself. This makes bargaining frustrating, because there's nothing for me to fix. You can't force someone to fall back in love with you, and you can't fix someone else. But I tried like a motherfucker.

**Depression, Reflection, Loneliness**   This was the theme for the month of March, and all three of them hit almost immediately.  As with most things in life, I used sarcasm to mask my pain.

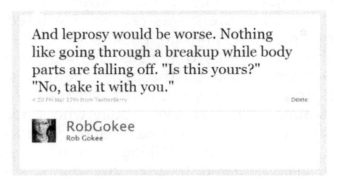

And leprosy would be worse. Nothing like going through a breakup while body parts are falling off. "Is this yours?" "No, take it with you."

4:20 PM Mar 27th from TwitterBerry        Delete

**RobGokee**
Rob Gokee

One of the problems I had fallen into in the five years previous to this month was a lack of close friends, friends that I could confide in.  I had very few people around me, and only one that I could really talk to, @kimberlyprendez, who was in the "Happy Relationship Place" & I didn't want to crap on her cereal.  I've known Kim for years, and she's been an amazing friend, but she was really my only friend.  My introversion had finally backfired on me.

I remember I jumped on Twitter that morning and posted a rather cryptic message about how the day was sucking.  Almost immediately I got a Direct Message (otherwise known as a DM on Twitter.  It's a private message you can send to and from people you follow and visa versa, no one else is privy to the information in it.) from this guy I'd just started following, @jamiefishback.  Jamie asked what was wrong, and I hesitated.  Not because he was an actor, although that should have been reason enough, but because I was trying to keep Twitter mostly professional, and this guy was asking me to open up.  But I was still in a state of shock, and I was desperate for someone to talk to, because the girlfriend was already on the phone with friends

66

talking about how it was all out in the open. So I decided to let Jamie be my friend and I told him. And he was there with a virtual hug and encouraging words, which surprised me. People didn't do that shit on MySpace. Why was Twitter any different? Jamie also offered to meet up for coffee and told me to keep him posted on how I was coping.

I didn't realize it at the time, but this moment was the turning point for Twitter and I. (I realize that, upon reading that statement, @jamiefishback's head will grow to the size of a large watermelon and burst with excitement, spewing seeds and pulp everywhere) He really was the catalyst for Twitter becoming "Not Just Another Social Network." That should be their tagline.

After I got off with Jamie, I was at a crossroads. I'd been tweeting with all these people I follow every day for months, and I wanted to tweet now about the things that were happening. My brain was consumed with the breakup, and that's all I wanted to talk about. But I was using Twitter to look for leads for film scoring, and I was pretty sure those people were not going to be interested in my drama.

The deciding factor ended up being my conversation with Jamie. I didn't really have anyone I could talk to, no one to get drunk with and drone on and on about what went wrong. But I had Twitter, the only social network I was actively participating in. So right here, at this desk, I made the decision to shift and tweet about my personal life on Twitter. If people were offended, or didn't want to deal with someone else's drama and depression, then screw them, they could unfollow me. I needed a place to vent, to rant, to whine about the huge event that was going on in my life.  And I did.

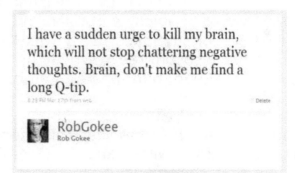

I have a sudden urge to kill my brain, which will not stop chattering negative thoughts. Brain, don't make me find a long Q-tip.

RobGokee
Rob Gokee

I didn't want to whine, I'd read enough tweets from people with problems who came off "whiny" on Twitter (I'm looking at you, @dr0id.), and it almost always came off way too emo to be mainstream.  My process was simple:  I wasn't trying to gain followers or purposely lose any; I just wanted to talk about how I was feeling.

Now, anyone who knows me (and those of you who have read this far into the book know me better than some people in real life do) knows that I'm sarcastic 98% of the time.  It's a trait that comes naturally, and I love being that way.  I try hard not to go too far over the edge, although there are times I do because it's necessary for the joke to work.  For instance, @Kevin Slack likes it when I send him pictures of me wearing just black socks. I don't know what he does with them, but he keeps asking for more and complains about the tendonitis in his right arm.

See?  Over the top.  Also, scary visual.

I am a very positive person, and I can find a bright spot in any situation, but my way of dealing with that is to make fun of it. Most of my tweets are a perfect example of that. I expected to lose a lot of followers when I started tweeting about the breakup. But something funny happened.

People listened.

Not only did they listen, they followed like mad and responded. It was the strangest thing I'd ever experienced. Here I was, my heart on the table for everyone to look at, and they weren't turning away. It was then I realized not only the secret of Twitter, but the power of Twitter.

When I say "secret," I don't mean that other book that's sold a gazillion copies. I mean that the "trick" to getting people to listen and interact on Twitter is to be human. Everyone has shitty things happen to them in their lives. People die, get cancer, divorce, cheat, and lose their jobs all the time. If you're relatable to everyone else, they see themselves in you, and you see yourself in them when they open up on Twitter. The heart of Twitter is not what you're selling, what your job is and who you know.

It's who you are.

Since this book is about who I am, let's keep going. As a special treat, I've arranged for @PostcardCoptors to bring you all refreshments during this part of the chapter because it's so long. If he hasn't knocked at your door with beer and/or wine by now, it means he drank it all single-handedly and is passed out at home, possibly urinating on himself. Dammit, Robert. You told me I could count on you this time.

## 11:11

I've neglected to mention that, during this month of mayhem, I still had to tweet from the set of the feature film "11:11." Every weekend in March we were shooting, and I had to talk about it. Breakup or no breakup. Yay me. So I went, and I tweeted.

I tweeted from Huntington Beach, from the park, from the inside of a house, everyplace we had to shoot. And I did it with the same snarkiness and sarcasm I had now employed to deal with the fact that my girlfriend already had a new place and was preparing to move by the end of the month.

People will tell you to find a distraction when intense, stressful events occur. It's a load of shit. There was no way for me to forget what was going on in my life by watching a movie being made. I will admit that there were times when I, either because I was laughing at something one of the PA's (Production Assistants) was doing (like flying a kite... literally) or because I was immersed in the shot Director Rocky Costanzo was getting (and I'd eventually be scoring), temporarily forgot that my life was so full of suckage I was suffocating. I'd be caught up in laughing and then suddenly I'd remember real life. It's a lot like when you wake up from a dream you thought was real, and then reality slowly seeps in and you
70

remember where you're at. I suppose if you were looking at my face during this moment of realization, you'd see the interesting transition from laughing to depression, like some creepy time lapse.

If you ask anyone, with the exception of Rocky (who I talked to about the situation), none of them were aware of what was going on. I'm very good at hiding that I'm stressed when I'm upset. I tend to get quiet, which is actually a huge warning sign that something is wrong, since I never shut up.

The girlfriend, after ending things, took a trip for about a week and I was alone at home, with WAY too much time to think about where she had gone, who lived there, and what they might be doing to each other. The first day was not bad. After taking her to the airport, I had a coffee meeting with a producer, and lunch & margaritas with another composer, @kevinrieplmusic. I slept fine, got up early and went to the set of 11:11 on the beach. It was a great day for it, and I was in a good mood.

Around 4 in the afternoon my imagination, which apparently had been napping all day, decided to wake up and kick into overdrive. All I could think about was what the ex was doing, who she might be doing it to, over and over and over in my head. I wanted to get away from the set, but I also didn't want to go home. I remember feeling antsy, like I was just going to explode into a million pieces right there at the craft services table, all over the bags of chips and vegetable platter. I was also taking the on-set photography that day, so not only did I have to be awake, I had to pay attention. When we wrapped at 8pm I bolted for my car and raced down highway home. I figured once I got there things would be better. I could not have been more wrong.

I couldn't sleep. I couldn't eat. I drank, but didn't get drunk. The thoughts of her were cancerous, spreading throughout my head and enveloping everything. I remember looking at the clock at midnight and thinking, OK, I've got to be on set at 8am, I should try and get some sleep. I thought the same thing at 2am when I was in the exact same spot. And again at 4am. I started contemplating the quickest way to find someone, anyone to have sex with, hoping it would make everything go away. Which was out of character for me. Not that I don't love sex. There's nothing like cuddling up with @jamiefishback on a bearskin rug, next to a roaring fire in a cabin.... but I digress. Sex, for me, is an emotional thing first, physical thing second. I need a connection with the person first or it just doesn't work for me. I realized this as I thought about where I could find someone to fill that hole (no pun intended) and make all the bad thoughts go away. I knew it wasn't going to make anything better, so instead I popped a handful of nighttime medication and passed out.

The next morning, which was actually about three hours later, was not any better. I woke up drenched in sweat, and it was air conditioned in my room. I stumbled to the set in a not-so-good mood and proceeded to tweet. And then people tweeted back. None of them had a clue about my night, I wasn't that specific about what was going on, I just talked about who was playing with themselves on set (Roy), who was drunk when we started shooting (Rocky) and who was tweeting lots of lies (Rob). But the thing is, the people of Twitter cared about what was going on in my life, even if I didn't. And my mood started to change. By the time we wrapped that day, which was the last day of shooting until the summer, I was laughing and feeling OK. This is a pic of me a few minutes before we wrapped production.

See? There's at least a half smile there. Yes, I was tweeting before and after this shot was taken by the illustrious Shawn Gorritz, @3quartermoon, who was the on set photographer for "11:11," who, knowing what I was going through that month, brought me the most amazing burrito all the way up from her home in San Diego.

In hindsight, maybe it was the burrito and not my followers that changed my mood. Sorry guys.

A week later, a strange thing happened when the ex-girlfriend got back into town (yes, I picked her up from the airport. I parked in the wrong terminal and had to walk across all of LAX, wondering why the hell I was there picking her up). When we hugged at the airport, it felt... strange. Like hugging your uncle Mort, or like when @heathvinyard goes in for a hug and puts his hands on your butt, and you want to say something, but you hesitate just a moment too long and then it's just easier to let it go.  I expected to miss her, to get emotional when I saw her, but I didn't.  It was like in one week apart she went from girlfriend to roommate, and I had no clue as to why.

During this time, I was also helping her furnish her new place with furniture and dishes.  I know what you're thinking.  Why the hell would I help her move out?!  It's because things were amicable at this point, and I still cared about her and didn't want her to have to do it all herself.  So we took a trip to Target.

The longer we're at Target, the more this is sucking. And not the good kind of sucking.

3:56 PM Mar 23rd from TwitterBerry          Delete

RobGokee
Rob Gokee

The trip to Target was not fun.  Not even close.  It started off OK, but then it just went downhill very quickly.  I very clearly remember a moment in Target when the ex-girlfriend took a phone call that was very clearly from the guy she'd been talking to and saw during her trip, walked away to take the call, and left me standing in front of the mini-blinds with a tape measure.  It was very much a "What The Fuck" moment.  I looked to my right and I found myself staring at a display of dishes and glassware.  I had this strong urge to walk over to sporting goods, grab a baseball bat, and destroy the display.  I thought about what all the different colors of glass would look like mixed together in a pile, broken and reflecting light.  I didn't do it, which is

74

good because then I'd have to wait in a jail cell for someone to come bail me out, and I don't think @ekfomo has that kind of cash on her during the weekend when the bars are open, so I'd be stuck in there with @TheUserPool, who'd be there without pants because, well, that's how he rolls. If I could do it over again, I'd still go to Target and help her pick out the things she needed, because, regardless of the situation, it was the right thing to do.

## Moving Day

Normally, a breakup is spread out a bit. You know it's coming, you've been fighting, things aren't going well, even if you *think* you didn't see it, you really saw it coming miles back down the highway. You know the spot, back when @farwyde was hitching a ride and you wanted to stop, but your girlfriend said "No, you are not picking up a hot girl hitchhiker," and you argue that she's not hot, but secretly you're hoping that your girlfriend will think she's hot too, and your girlfriend says, "Maybe she's a serial killer, you should be thanking me," but all you hear is "blah blah blah hot girl blah blah blah," and you can't get in a word edgewise and before you know it you end up at Trader Joe's picking out wine for dinner at your girlfriend's parents house, where you'll spend the night wondering about the lucky bastard that pulled over instead of you and gave @farwyde a ride, and how it had better not be that sonofabitch @TheUserPool, because he's only got one thing on his mind 24/7.

Where was I? Oh yeah. Moving. The day the movers came and took her stuff away was very.... weird.

> If you're a Mormon going door to door, the worst time to come to my door is today. And if I say no, you probably shouldn't push it.
>
> 1:18 PM Mar 30th from TwitterBerry · Delete
>
> **RobGokee**
> Rob Gokee

The two weeks between her getting back and moving day were up and down emotionally. I was OK around her most of the time, and slept (somewhat), although I still wasn't eating almost at all, which is how I cope with stress. It's the most effective diet plan I've ever been on (and the only one). Yes, I realize it's incredibly unhealthy, but it's not like I was hungry and refusing to eat. I wasn't hungry. I was digesting the big ball of stress sitting in my stomach instead. The two trips to Target happened during this period, but, despite this, I felt emotionally that I was ready for her to move.

I wasn't.

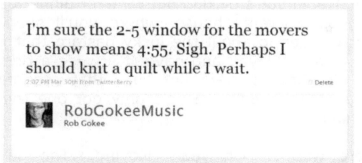

> I'm sure the 2-5 window for the movers to show means 4:55. Sigh. Perhaps I should knit a quilt while I wait.
>
> 2:07 PM Mar 30th from TwitterBerry · Delete
>
> **RobGokeeMusic**
> Rob Gokee

When I got up the morning of the 30th, I was ready. All her stuff was packed, the movers were coming, we just had to get all the boxes near the door and load up her car with the stuff she didn't want on the truck. But something happened. I didn't realize it, but I was slowly getting angry for the first time since it all went down on March 4th. I rarely get mad, and when I do I get real quiet. It's like my stress response, but... angrier. Not yell/scream/break things kind of mad, because I don't get mad like that, I internalize. And not in a physical way either, I've never laid a hand on a woman, and aliens would literally have erupted from my asshole before that would ever happen in any situation. I wasn't mad at her, I was mad at the situation and that it had actually come to this, the end. I mean, what the fuck, universe? Really? Am I really watching 4 1/2 years of my life come to an end in less than 30 days? I was mad at the relationship. I suppose I should have been mad at the asshole that was taking her away from me. But if it wasn't him, it would have been someone else, because she was ready to move on regardless. So instead, I was angry at the relationship itself. With no one to take it out on.

Then the Mormons came to the door.

Now I don't have anything against any religion. I think people should be free to believe whatever they want to believe as long as they're not hurting anyone in the process. I do, however, have a problem with pushy salespeople. And really, that's what they were there to do, sell me some religion. I heard a knock at the door and walked over to the stairs (they look down to the front door) and I could see them through the screen. I very calmly said, "This is the worst possible day for you to be here. You need to leave now."

If they had left, there would have been no incident. But one of them said, "Are you sure you don't have a minute to talk? Can we come back another day?" Really, it could have been anyone at the door. The UPS guy, the mailman, a creepy old man selling candy. But it was the guy trying to sell me religion who took the brunt of my anger over the end of my relationship.

"What part of get the fuck off my porch did you not understand?"

I started yelling. And cursing. Loudly. There was a moment when they started to go, and one of them turned to say something. I haven't been in a fight since I was 10. But I was SO ready to punch him in the face if he said one word to me. Fortunately for both of us, he turned and left.

And I felt better.

In hindsight, I should have gone into the bedroom and yelled at the wall hours before that happened, it would have helped me get it all out. Unfortunately, that guy had to take the brunt of it. I felt bad, but at the same time it was cathartic to get it out.

That was also the point when the sadness hit harder than @os1019 when you insult his cooking. He's very sensitive about it; entire legions of men have been wiped out because of an insult to his culinary prowess. OK, that *might* be a lie. @os1019 has been a great friend throughout the entire year, was there before March reared its ugly head, and is still my friend now.

Well, as much a friend as he can be since he's a cyborg.

Much like @thebookjournal. She'll tell you she's human, but there is no way a human can read as much as she does. One day I'm going to find her wiring harness and proclaim "AH HA!" And then she'll vaporize me while @os1019 looks on.

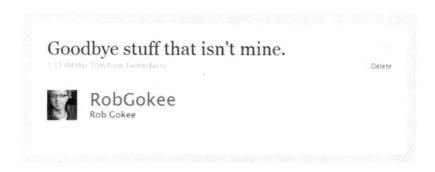

Goodbye stuff that isn't mine.

3 13 PM Mar 30th from TwitterBerry                    Delete

RobGokee
Rob Gokee

Then the movers showed up.

I was starting to feel really shitty really fast. I'm not afraid to cry. There are movies and TV shows that bring tears to my eyes (the episode "The Body" from Buffy chokes me up every single time I watch it), but there had been very little crying the month of March. I remember there were tears on the 4th, the day everything ended, but none in-between. I'd been running at full speed all month, helping her pack, changing over utilities, working from the set of the film, I didn't let myself slow down and grieve, because I was afraid to.

What took 4 and 1/2 years to accumulate took about 20 minutes to load into a truck in front of the house. It was so fast, suddenly we were hugging at the top of the stairs, and she walked out the door. I can't remember any time in my life that I felt more alone, unloved, and the smallest I've ever been. It was the last time she ever set foot in the apartment. I remember like it was yesterday, I walked past the dining room, through the living room to the bedroom. I stood in the corner facing out, leaned back and tweeted.

And then I slid down the wall and cried. For a long time.

# Chapter 8: April 2009
## Rum, Pants & @cartermason: A Guide to Corner Turning

See, this is why I don't save things. I don't need to find memorabilia from our vacation to Monterey. Or sticky notes expressing emotion.

6:26 PM Apr 1st, 2009 from TwitterBerry     Delete

robgokee
Rob Gokee

April did not start off with a bang. It was really just cancerous March seeping in underneath the April door. I'd pretty much stopped eating and socializing after Moving Day. A breakup ended up being the best diet I'd ever been on, because the small amount of fat that had accumulated on my abs had melted off without exercise. I was eating like one meal a day.

Oh, it's OK, don't worry. I made up for it by drinking.

When you live with someone for 4+ years, and in one month, without warning, they're gone, it's a tremendous shock, and the house is quieter than you'd ever imagine. I'd turn on TV and radio in every room of the house just for the noise. I'd just

81

vegetate for hours at a time, realize I was hungry, make food and stop eating after two bites because I was nauseated.

I really had one person who I could talk to, @kimberlyprendez. Kim and I went back years, and she too had gone through horrible relationship problems when I was one of the only people she could confide in. She's an incredible listener, even when I ramble. She's my best friend, (aside from one other person), and was really my first therapist. It's convenient that she's so good at it, because she's in school right now to become a real one.

I realized, after talking with Kim, that I also needed to talk to a therapist. So I called one.

Cranking Good Charlotte and trying to figure out what the hell I'm doing with the rest of my day. That's right, Hell. I cursed. Dammit.

10:35 AM Apr 5th, 2009 from TwitterBerry                    Delete

robgokee
Rob Gokee

I'd been to a therapist once as a teen. My parents were having some issues, my mom and I weren't getting along, and so I saw some guy two or three times. It was an OK experience, there was no couch and he didn't speak with a foreign accent. He was more like Mr. Rogers. I think it's akin to meeting @cartermason for the first time. You feel comfortable, despite the smell of alcohol on his breath, you're talking, laughing, and then WHAM, suddenly you wake up in a bathtub full of ice and a missing liver. Carter is a great guy, and one of my best friends. You'll be reading about how we met soon enough. It was a "being in the same emotional place at the same time" kind of thing. A bromance.

SO, therapy. I wanted to go to therapy. I'd had friends that went to therapy, I was always slightly jealous that they got to spill their life's problems to someone who HAD to listen.

Mostly because they were paid to.

It was a good time for me to go. I'd had three major relationships in my life, and two of them ended the same way. I needed to know if there was a common thread, something I was doing without being aware, something I was missing so that I could fix it before I allowed myself to be in the position where I would let someone inside and fall in love again.

I went to a place with multiple therapists at one office. Like a pack of Skittles, you just kind of close your eyes and put one in your mouth. OK, maybe not like a pack of Skittles. This metaphor thing is harder than it looks. More like a police lineup. There was one problem though.

The first person I picked out of the lineup was not a tasty Skittle. No, it was definitely a shit-flavored Skittle.

If I wanted to write a contrived, stereotypical character into a screenplay who was a psychologist, it would have been this guy. He had a strong accent that made him hard to understand. He blamed everything on my adoption, claiming I had abandonment issues. He pulled photocopied sheets for me to "study from" like he had a fucking lesson plan. This was all in the first session. I mentioned Twitter and he shook his head and told me the internet was "no good." Yes, that's a quote. Each session (and there were only three), he let me talk for about 10 minutes, and then *he* talked the rest of the session. He also quoted Freud. Seriously. The straw that broke the camel's back was the third session when he mixed me up with another patient. I had no problem walking out at the end of the session to the reception desk and saying "I need to switch to a competent therapist, please. NOW."

I switched to a female therapist. My best friend in high school, Michele, was a girl. I've always felt more comfortable opening up to a woman over a man. Unless we're talking about @roomtone. But that's because he wears a dress. And lipstick.

I showed up to meet Skittle #2 the first week of April. The first thing I noticed was that she was not ugly, and I immediately worried that this would be a distraction. It was not. She also told me that I was in charge of what we talked about, and to start wherever I wanted.

She was SO hired.

I knew 15 minutes in that I was going to be comfortable telling her anything, and that there'd be no judgment from her. She'd even heard of Twitter.

Going to therapy was great, but after it was over I still had to come back to an empty bedroom. One of those nights in April is where Pantsless was born.

84

When I'm done with you, Wednesday,
I'm going to throw your carcass next to
Monday & Tuesday, who are slumped in
the corner.

robgokee
Rob Gokee

## The Pants Come Off

One night I was making pasta and shrimp for dinner. It was a good night so far, and I was in a somewhat good mood. I remember I was flipping shrimp in a skillet, when suddenly my brain, in a split second, went to that place where you're imagining the person you used to be intimate with having sex with someone else.

It's a wonderful feeling, having those thoughts.

It's like going somewhere with @dr0id. You think you're going to the movies to see Avatar for the 8th time, but without warning he pulls up to some abandoned ride at Coney Island, where there's a clown face on the entrance all melted from years of rain, old condom wrappers, syringes scattered in front of the ticket counter, and a toothless man with no pants peeing on the clown face's mouth. That's pretty much the same feeling you get when you're imagining someone you used to love "doing" someone else on a loop in your head, with audio.

I put down the spatula, turned off the burner, and walked into the bedroom to get my hoodie and Blackberry. Only one thing was going to purge the cancerous images from my unrelenting & loud head.

85

Rum.

Calm down, @thewallsaresoft. She likes rum so much she keeps the empty bottles and names them like children.

The picture above is me just before I walked out the door, up the street to the liquor store, bought rum, and walked home. I was officially in a shitty mood.

I sat on the bed, made a rum and coke (more rum than coke), turned up the stereo and tweeted. It was the first time I'd tweeted drunk, I was still very much in a place where I didn't care if I lost followers for saying something inappropriate (actually, I still feel that way. But now it's for different reasons), I just needed to vent.

AND vent I did.

At one point someone asked me where I was tweeting from.  My response was this:

> Drunk Rob is singing Sugar, We're Going Down while tweeting. And juggling balls, while breathing fire & Tweeting. Dressed like a sad clown.

robgokee
Rob Gokee

A few minutes later I decided to expand upon the joke.  I included the word "pantsless."  It was funny, and totally untrue since I was blasting Fall Out Boy as loud as I could in bed, clothed, the pint of rum gone in less than an hour.  I drank it faster than @boriser shoots a film.  Hmm.  That was a compliment. I was really looking for an insult.  Let me try again. I drank it faster than @ekfomo can say "Cheers!"

The thing that surprised me is that everyone was into it, asking questions; enjoying my misery (I mean that in a good way, I was enjoying it, too). Also, I was gaining followers hourly in droves. I didn't know why. A lot of them were filmmakers. Why wasn't everyone ignoring the depressed guy who wouldn't shut up?

That's the thing about marketing yourself on Twitter.

People will talk to you and follow you even if you're fallible.  That's the key to gaining and keeping followers, and the key to turning them into friends, associates, and possibly customers. **Being Yourself.**

Being yourself will take you further on Twitter than any gimmick or pitch.

There are limitations. You have to carefully ride the line between (for instance) scandalous and perverted. If you're doing depressed on Twitter like I did, it helps to make fun of yourself at the same time. I have always masked my pain with humor, for so long that it's a part of who I am. Some people don't do sarcasm, both giving and receiving; you'll lose some people who don't get that kind of humor. You just have to commit to it and stay your course, or you'll look fake, and people will know it.

Here's an example, but it's not a tweet. I wrote two "stories" during April. The first one was actually a chat one day when I went off on a tangent, and then posted it to my Facebook, which I had rejoined to torture myself. It's a very happy story. Really.

## Picture's Sorrow

*The loss of Picture's baby was tragic, she was taking it harder than anyone expected. Perhaps if Picture had been more careful around the fireplace, her baby would still be with her. "Wood and fire don't mix," she told herself as she sobbed quietly, rocking back and forth, looking very small & alone in the corner.*

*Picture looked down at the cracks in her frame and cursed softly. She didn't care; she wanted to be placed in a quiet hallway of the house, the far end of the hallway that never saw the sun's rays, a picture of a small puppy shivering outside in the rain placed inside.*

*What happened next seemed to be in slow motion, at least to Picture. She never saw the baseball come through the open window, a victim of Tommy Jarvis' wild left arm. Then she saw the ball coming at her, spiraling slowly. The stitching on the ball looked like a mouth, screaming at her as it landed on her glass front. There was a moment of silence, Picture could hear nothing but a bird chirping outside, and smelled the tulips outside the window. Then her glass shattered explosively, shards of her body flying in every direction. There was a flash of pain, Picture thought it reminded her of the time John put a nail in her frame, and then, suddenly, she felt nothing.*

*Picture looked down sadly at her wooden frame, which was now in three pieces. I still feel whole, she thought, and wondered if this was what her mother had felt when she had been killed in that tornado years prior. Picture tried to take a breath, but she couldn't inhale well, which was mostly due to the fact that she didn't have any lungs. She closed her eyes and, for a second, was relieved that her pain would now go away. Then she died.*

*Then a clown burst into the room, squirting water at everything from a broach and honking a horn with his butt.*

The second one came a week later. Don't worry, it's more comedic than the last one (shakes head no).

**A Flower For Prudence**

Prudence had always been aware she was a vase. The fact that people kept putting flowers in her gave it away, and she was made of high quality ceramic. Prudence looked down at the dead roses inside her. Most of the petals had fallen off and were floating in the water, which had begun to stagnate. Prudence peered over the edge of the China cabinet she was perched on. She could see the body of Susan Summers on the floor below. Prudence had belonged to Susan for over three decades, and knew she was dead. At 93, Susan's heart attack had been inevitable, and Prudence watched in horror as her only friend collapsed last Friday night while reaching for her tea. For a few hours, Susan twitched. Prudence wished she'd been made with arms and hands so she could call for help, but Prudence knew the window of opportunity for that had now closed.

It had been almost a week, and no one had come to the house. Prudence was glad she was a vase, and didn't have a nose, she knew the smell of Susan's decaying body would be unbearable at this point. Susan had outlived most of her family and children and no one had visited her in months. Even the mail had begun to pile up in front of the door, just below the rusty slot that creaked every time mail arrived.

Prudence wondered what would become of her now that Susan was gone. She imagined men coming in and clearing out all the "junk." Prudence imagined herself being tipped upside down and emptied, and then tossed in a bin with the other trash. It was an almost comforting thought, she was tired. Tired of being a vessel, tired of being filled with other's broken promises and fake apologies. Prudence wished she could throw herself from the China cabinet, and land next to Susan's head, shattered in dozens of pieces but finally at peace. But she

90

*couldn't, so she'd have to be content with sitting there indefinitely, until the day the house was emptied by strange hands, and she was discarded. Then a clown with floppy ears came into the room, riding a unicycle and juggling pies.*

What is it with me and clowns? (Scratches head). I should probably bring that up in therapy. Anyway, I tweeted drunk. And I felt better. And more people followed. Good people, people who cared and asked questions and commiserated with me. Not @GraphikDeziner. She pointed and laughed. She even spit. Not really, she's actually an amazing graphic designer named Jenny who almost illustrated this book, except that she's so good she's swamped, and I have enough pictures in here already I realized if we added more we might as well make this a pop-up book. But you can see her stuff at www.bandwagongraphiks.com. She also bike rides like a gazillion miles a day.

What? That's a number.

## Meetings

Working, working, working, working. This had better monetize itself at some point.

3:03 PM Apr 15th, 2009 from TweetDeck                    Delete

robgokee
Rob Gokee

On top of that, this other weird thing happened in April. Filmmakers I'd been talking to and schmoozing for months and months suddenly wanted to meet to talk about scoring projects. One of them was @JonathanNail. Jonathan is one of the funniest, animated guys you'll meet. He's an actor, he's been on Mad Men and Carnivale, but he's also a writer. He even wrote a blurb for the back of this book. Go look, I'll wait.

He was working on a webseries about a guy stuck in space on his way to Mars. We met for lunch, I hadn't read the script yet, and he pitched his ass off right there at the table. He was acting out parts, flailing his limbs and shouting out lines. Once I realized he wasn't having a stroke, I was intrigued. I went home, read the script and almost peed my pants with laughter. Like when @brownambassador is tickling you, and you're laughing so hard you can't breathe, and then he starts tickling your inner thigh and it feels... different... and then... Wait, this doesn't happen to you guys? Just me? Hmm.

I emailed @JonathanNail and practically fell over myself wanting to score the project.

And I am. And it's because of Twitter.

There was another filmmaker I met with during the same week, a Twitter person I'd been talking to semi-regularly. Little did I know he'd become far more than a business associate. Unless you consider drinking "business." His name?

Carter Mason.

You have to say it like that, too; you can't just say "Carter." There's like a law, you can be arrested for not saying it properly in five states. Think of it like Jack Bauer.

Carter is a writer/director and an actor as well. Carter and I had been talking on Twitter, I was feeling a little cocky after the @JonathanNail meeting for @SOLOtheSeries, so I scheduled a meeting with Carter (I'm allowed to abbreviate his name, by the way, I got permission from the man himself) to talk about his short film that needed music. We met at a bar called Big Wang's in North Hollywood.

Later I would remark that it was a fitting place for us to meet.

I didn't know it at the time, but Carter was going through a breakup of his own. We met after he had played a softball game (not an adult league, he used to crash little league games and force his way onto the mound to pitch), and he was already a little inebriated by the time I got there. And I was perturbed.

Perturbed that I wasn't already drunk, too.

I grabbed a beer and we started talking about the film, we watched it right there at the table on his laptop. But then we switched the conversation to relationships, and found that we were both in a slump. Now, I've said that @kimberlyprendez is a great friend. An AMAZING friend. But she was in a happy place full of flowers and bunnies, whereas I was full of crab grass and bunny shit. Although she was a great ear, I needed to talk to someone else who was in the dark place. After meeting Carter, I realized how nice it was to have someone to confide in that knew how it felt.

Carter and I had like a four hour "meeting" at the bar. We talked incessantly about ex-girlfriends, drunken escapades, films, upbringing, it was an

instant bromance. I'd like to think it helped us both.
Carter and I are still friends; he even got back together with his girlfriend and they moved in together.

What about me, you ask? I never found anyone; I decided to stay single, collecting locks of hair from supermodels and building model airplanes. And I wrote a book.

After that last statement, I can hear some of you yelling "Liar!", while others of you are yelling "Cheers!" (shut up, @ekfomo) and other things not fit for print. Yes, @jasonburns, I can hear you. Fine, it's possible that I met a new friend that happened to be female, but that's a boring story, and really not fit for this book. I think it's much more appropriate at this juncture in the book to talk about the health care crisis in this country, and what steps we need to take to remedy the debt we're accumulating.

Hey, don't get mad. It's not like I met her on Twitter or anything.

# Chapter 9: May 2009
## Meet @alliecine

@alliecine I had your house moved
while you were gone. Now it's just a dirt
lot. Good luck finding it.

10:43 PM Apr 3rd, 2009 from TweetDeck in reply to alliecine                    Delete

robgokeemusic
Rob Gokee

If you're lucky, there are times in your life when someone comes along who changes everything for you. Usually, it's when you least expect it. This chapter, and the month of May 2009, is about that person. But let's backtrack a bit.

Back in December 2008, I added lots of new followers on Twitter. One of them was a producer whose username was @alliecine. We didn't really chat much at that point, neither of us were tweeting a ton yet, and I didn't know her from anyone else on the site. I think I found her on Twellow when I was doing filmmaker searches for people to follow.

Perhaps it was her avatar at the time that seduced –
I mean interested – me.

Speaking of avatars, here is the progression of mine
over my first year on Twitter.

I suppose it would have been more drastic if some of
my avatars had hair and then there was some
progression from hair to no hair, but the "no hair"
thing was really an overnight whim that involved me
and a razor. Occasionally I think about growing it
back, but I'm so used to it by now I think it'd be
weird to have it back. Also, when I'm under
@kevinrieplmusic's desk, he likes to rub it while I....
nevermind.

It's important, especially if you're selling something
or yourself on Twitter, that you stay somewhat
consistent with your avatar. Your followers will get
used to seeing what you look like, and if you change
the avatar, it throws them off for a bit. If your

Twitter account is a personal account, it's not a big a deal. But if you're a business of some kind (even porn stars, I don't want @ce54r feeling left out), you want your customers to find you, and you want to "brand" yourself. Try and keep avatar changes to a minimum.

OK, back to me.

In March 2009 (three months prior), I got an email from @alliecine. She'd come across a lead for a scoring job and wanted to pass it on to me. I was surprised; it was the first time Twitter had potentially monetized itself. It was the first lead I'd received, and unsolicited at that. I emailed the director she recommended (For the record, I didn't get the gig; I don't even remember what film it was at this point. I'm sure the film suffered because I didn't score it. Yeah, I'm cocky like that.), but I decided I should meet this @alliecine person and find out what she did in the industry so I could recommend her as well, and maybe get some more work out of her. We set up a coffee meeting in North Hollywood at the Coffee Bean on Lankershim and Chandler at 11am, Friday, March 13th.

If you've been paying attention, you'll remember that March was not a great month. For anything.

The ex-girlfriend and I spent the week before my meeting with @alliecine talking about whether things were fixable and if she was interested in working things out. The 12th of March it was decided (not by me) that it was definitely over. The next day, I took her to the airport for a trip to the Midwest that she'd planned the month before, and I went straight from LAX to my meeting with @alliecine.

I've always said, in hindsight, that the timing of that meeting was not the greatest. I was really not in a place of creativity and taking on new work, I was in a place of wallowing and rum. But because I never say no, I took the meeting. Ask @angelobell about my inability to say "No." I've scored like eight projects for the man, including the feature "Broken Hearts Club," where I had to write 80 minutes of music in 10 days. Don't get me wrong, I love it when the stakes are high and the time is short. My best scoring comes from those kinds of projects.

But, after writing this chapter of the book, I've realized that the timing could not have been more perfect. It was the epitome of "one door closes, another one opens." It just took me a few months to figure it out.

I remember the meeting like it was yesterday. I was early, since I came right from the airport, she was slightly late. We sat outside, right next to a location where a film crew was shooting.

And we talked... about business the entire time.

It was a one hour meeting that lasted 2 ½ hours. We covered my projects, hers, how long we'd been in the industry, the only "personal" conversation we had was where we'd grown up. I'm wordy, and with

98

coffee I'm really wordy, but she was matching me in the convo.

But there was no flirting. Because of where I was emotionally, I approached the meeting without any agenda, no "rebound" thoughts, no ulterior motive. I do remember thinking she was a beautiful woman, but I reminded myself why I was there and kept the convo on the topic of film and music.

At some point, locked in conversation, I remembered I had a lunch with @kevinrieplmusic. It had already been over two hours, and it felt like five minutes. I wanted to skip the lunch with Kevin so I could keep talking to her. Fortunately for Kevin, I didn't. I waited until the last possible moment to leave, with literally 10 minutes to get to my car and drive two cities away. We said our goodbyes, and vowed to keep in touch.

I made the lunch on time. It was a "wallow in a sea of margaritas over my breakup" kind of lunch at Casa Vega. Kevin's a good friend. And almost as good a composer as I am. Almost.

After that, @alliecine and I started tweeting back-and-forth on a regular basis, and more than I was tweeting with anyone else. It's not so much that I was smitten with her (yet). I was still in a bad place relationship-wise, and not thinking at all about finding someone new. She was just so damned interesting, and had more things going on at one time than I did, which I didn't think possible. She was also hot, and I had to concentrate not to drool on myself, or at least hide it well. She was more driven to succeed than any woman I'd ever met. And that was both interesting and incredibly sexy at the same time.

Our tweeting was, in hindsight, like two 5th graders on the playground who call each other names because they're not smart enough to figure out how to tell the other person they like them.

OK, maybe that was more me than her.

The above tweets are a good example of how @alliecine and I communicated. And because of our near-constant interactions (I didn't write squat musically in May, I'd stopped looking for scoring work in March and was content spending all my time thinking about how miserable I was), I started to gain followers, some of hers and some just from the fact that I was tweeting A LOT, and more of it was from interacting with other people rather than talking about myself, something I still do today. But make no mistake, I was still miserable. Talking to @alliecine made it slightly more bearable. Unlike taking to @christinacheney, which leaves me feeling like I'm leaving the interaction with an Apple sticker stuck on my butt and, during the conversation, she had goons break in my studio and destroy my PC.

@alliecine and I started talking by Facebook chat as well, and then we moved to AIM. It became a nightly ritual, talking to her at 11pm for an hour or so, going on about our day until one or the other of us passed out. She used to chat on her laptop sideways, lying on her bed, and would occasionally just stop chatting because she fell asleep. It was cute.

No, she did not fall asleep because of the conversation.

I was fascinated by her; I'd never met anyone going 200 mph that still managed to get stuff done really well. I am very much a juggler when it comes to work. I love my ToDo List. There is never a time when my ToDo List is empty. By the time I finish things, I'm already thinking about what I want and need to do next. She worked the same way. Sure, I've worked with lots of driven people. But everyone has there own way of proceeding with projects and getting things done, and Allie was the first person I'd come across that did it the same way I did.

By the time May reared its ugly head, I had a problem.

We'd become friends. I was starting to feel comfortable confiding in her, in a way I didn't confide in other people. And I was talking about her to @kimberlyprendez all the time.

**Me**: And then Allie said this, and I said that, and then SHE said this, and I laughed. And then SHE laughed. (pause) You had to be there.
Kim: You've got a crush on her.

**Me**: Yeah, right. That's ridiculous.

Kim: Are you stupid?

**Me**: NO.

Kim: You are if you don't realize you have a crush on her. You talk about her all the time. You talk TO her all the time.

**Me**: No I don't. We chat in the morning when we get up, then we tweet during the day, and then we chat for a few hours at night, but that's it.

Kim: Mmhmm.

**Me**: OMG, that's exactly what Allison says! And then I say-

Kim: You are SO crushing on her. HARD.

**Me**: Shit.

Kim: Tell her.

**Me**: And screw up the friendship? No way. I'll get over it. I don't think she feels the same way.

Kim: She's in Europe with her sister for 2 weeks, right?

**Me**: Yeah.

Kim: How often do you talk to her?

**Me**: We email once a day.

Kim: How many of her guy friends do you think she's emailing with while she's in Europe for the first time?

**Me**: (meekly) All of them? (pause) That doesn't mean she feels the same way.

Kim: It's amazing you ever dated anyone in your entire life.

**Me**: I don't have to take this abuse.

Kim: It's time. Ask her out.

I wasn't sure yet. Then, a few days later, at 2am in morning, Allison texted me from the Dallas airport during a four hour layover. We chatted until almost 6am, and I realized that she wouldn't be talking to me for this long, at this time of the day, if she wasn't interested. So I asked her out.

Kind of.

I wasn't very clear that it was a "date," even though said "outing" was dinner and a movie.

Yeah, I was that dense.

In any case, two days after she got back, we went on our "date." I called Kim on the way to Allie's house and she told me I had to find out, before the night was over, if this was really a "date." We went to PF Chang's for dinner and saw "Star Trek." Then we went back to her apartment and...

Talked. For about four more hours.

It was literally an eight hour first date. I talk a lot. When I'm nervous, I talk fast. It's a lethal combination. But Allison talks fast too, so there was this surreal moment on the couch when we were immersed in conversation, both of us weaving in and out and going a million miles a minute, when I realized that she was the female version of me.

I also realized, about seven hours into the date, that I still hadn't determined whether or not it was a date. So I decided to lay it all on the line.

**Me**: Yo, baby. You so fine, you wanna be my boo?
Allie: (blank stare)
**Me**: Don't leave me hanging, baby, gimme a little sugar.
Allie: (reaches for gun)

OK, it didn't go quite like that. I told her how I felt about her, and she told me the feeling was mutual. I was overjoyed.

But there was a problem.

It was at that moment I realized there were some things we hadn't discussed that we really, really needed to discuss. Like the small, insignificant, not really important fact that there was a teenage boy living with me, a teenager that shared my genetic imprint.

Like I said; nothing important.

*Author's Note: This next section of the book is brought to you by @alliecine, who thought it should be included. At first I said no, and then she persuaded me by holding a pillow over my head until I started to twitch, which convinced me that she was right. None of this appeared on Twitter, so you're getting the exclusive scoop right here.*

There were two reasons this never came up in conversation.

First, during business meetings, I don't talk about family unless it comes up directly. It's not that I'm ashamed of my family; it's that I try to separate the two. When you're applying for a job, family is not the first thing you talk about, sometimes it doesn't even come up until after you're hired, and a lot people don't like to mix the two. I've worked with over 50 directors in my job as a composer, and a good lot of them don't even know that I was married or have children. But I don't know personal details about them either. It's just the way it works when you freelance and you have different bosses that come and go quickly. Some people I work with I become friends with, and then that kind of stuff comes out as you get to know them personally. Like @1111Movie's Rocky Costanzo. We've spent hours and hours talking about relationships and life, things that had nothing to do with the score we were working on together. Very few people know that Rocky has five wives and 16 children scattered all over the country. I told him I'd never tell a soul.

The second reason I hadn't said anything about kids is... well, it's a ridiculous reason. When you're a single father and you're dating, two things generally happen. You either have the women who think it's admirable that you're raising your kids and date you, or the ones that are like "You have children? I've gotta go." There was a point during which I realized I was crushing on @alliecine and that the topic of children hadn't come up "naturally." My brain decided, in its infinite wisdom, that there was no reason to rush telling her. We weren't dating; we were still "composer" and "producer." It didn't really matter if we were just friends as long as you didn't lie about it if she asked you directly.

I listened to that part of my brain.

Fast forward to the first "date," and literally the moment I realized we were actually on a date. Then THAT stupid part of my brain was like, "Yo, man, I gotta go. I got some things to take care of, peace out."

Then the logical part of my brain, which clearly had been on vacation, showed up, suitcase still in his hand and lei around his neck going "What the hell is going on here? Who made this mess? You didn't tell her about the kid? What were you thinking? I'm gone for a month and this is what happens?!"

So I told her. And she was shocked. Not that I had kids, that part of the whole scenario, ironically, didn't make any difference in the way that she felt about me, which is something I should have already guessed. The part that shocked her was the fact that I'd been keeping it from her.

I didn't make any excuses, I told her how it had happened, why, and took full responsibility for screwing it up. On top of everything else, I didn't want her to think I was lying to get out of it. She listened and nodded, and said she needed some time to process the information. I said "I understand."

And the next day, she said we shouldn't date anymore.

# Chapter 10: June 2009
## Extroversion Grabs Me By The...Hair

I need to break out of the strange funk
I'm in today, which is frustrating
because I don't know what's causing it.
Maybe it's menopause.

12:12 PM May 30th, 2009 from TweetDeck                                    Delete

 robgokee
Rob Gokee

The End.

That's it, that's the end of the book. I swear, the
rest of the pages are blank. Thank you for reading,
we have cupcakes and punch in the back of the room
as you exit. Please take a complimentary copy of
*The Secret* on your way out, we're trying to get rid of
them.

Goodbye.

You're still here aren't you?  You're expecting some sort of resolution to the whole "Allison" thing, huh?

Fine.  But I can't guarantee I'm going to remember where I was.

I had fucked up.  I can't think of a non-curse word that conveys how I I felt about the situation.  I didn't blame @alliecine for not wanting to date.  I knew I was falling for her a while before I asked her out.  I realized there were kid-related things I hadn't told her, and that I should have brought them up before I asked her out.  But there was this very illogical part of my brain that was telling me to wait for the "right opportunity" to talk about it.

Let me tell you right now, there is no "right opportunity."  If you're in the same situation, whether it's now or in the future, take it from me, no matter what your heart is telling you in order to protect it from being broken, listen to your head.  Your heart is NEVER going to let you talk about it, but your head knows better.

So we went back to being friends, although now it was with the knowledge that I'd blown something potentially really, really good.  @alliecine's birthday was the next week, and I'd ordered a cheesecake from Junior's all the way on the East Coast (where she is from), and had it shipped here, and I told her I still wanted to give it to her.  Part of me wanted to eat the whole thing myself in bed while watching multiple episodes of *House*, but I decided the right thing to do was give it to her.  Allie suggested I bring it over and we could get some dinner.

On the way to her house, I called @kimberlyprendez and talked about ALL the reasons it was good that @alliecine and I weren't dating. There were like three, and they weren't even good reasons. I knocked on her door, trying to tell myself that she would make a better friend than girlfriend, and then she opened the door. She looked so beautiful standing there; all I wanted to do was bang my head against the wall in frustration.

We went to the Italian restaurant up the street, and it just about killed me to be around her, because all I could think about was that I'd blown it. I pretended to be OK with being friends, but inside I was kicking my own ass on repeat.

> Rob: This ends now. (Starts to make Bed.) Bed: What are you doing?! Stop, we're friends, remember? It doesn't have to be this way!

robgokee
Rob Gokee

We scaled back on our conversations, but still talked on Twitter. One night the following week she randomly chatted me. I don't remember the date or time, I'm not one to keep track of those kinds of things.

### June 3rd, 11:03pm.

It had been about a week and a half, I was working on moving toward the notion that we were done. More done than @mocoddle after a blog post. That analogy works because @mocoddle pours so much into each post she's drained afterward. I realize, in order for that to work, you'd have to have read her blog. What are you waiting for? Also, she farms cows on the moon. It's her day job, she's not really enamored with it, as the cows keep floating away, and trying to milk a cow in space is a whole other "thing." Add to that the lack of health benefits (and gravity), and you can see why she gives her all to her blog instead. Where was I?

I was just impressed by what @KimberlyPrendez wrote for our new website. If you're not following her, you should be. She tweets naked.

1:22 PM Jul 29th, 2009 from web          Delete

 robgokee
Rob Gokee

@alliecine and I were chatting, making small talk, and then, faster than I can shuck a pair of pants, she told me she wasn't over me and unsure of what to do about it. I immediately recalled (in my head) a conversation I'd had with @kimberlyprendez a few days prior.

Kim: Wassup?
**Me:** Nothin.
Kim: Then why the hell did you call me? I have a life too, you know. I was organizing paper clips.
**Me:** I think I'm doing better with this @alliecine debacle.
Kim: Really?
**Me:** No.
Kim: It'll get better as time goes on blahblahblahblahblahblahblah (This isn't what she

said. This is how I heard it in my head. Kim likes to ramble.)

**Me:** Mmhmm.

Kim: Are you even listening to me? You'd better have pants on.

**Me:** Of course I do (I didn't). I'm glad she and I are still friends, but it's incredibly hard to pretend I don't have feelings for her. My standards have changed; I only want someone that's as good as she is. I don't know if I'll ever find that again.

Kim: Hypothetically, if like 4 years went by, and then @alliecine showed up and told you she wanted you back--

**Me:** I'd do it in a heartbeat. I don't care where I am or what's going on.

Kim: Wow.

**Me:** Totally.

Clearly I was not over her. There was something about @alliecine that I hadn't seen in anyone I'd ever dated. We thought alike, and solved problems the same way; we literally had hundreds of things in common. It was almost like we shared the same brain.

She clearly had the logical part of it.

@alliecine RLOL (squints) stop trying to entice me with random violence & jokes. Don't make me come over there.

robgokee
Rob Gokee

I was in shock for a few moments; it's a lot like the moment when you realize that @ginayates is really serious when she tells you that wants to be on Law &

Order. She's quite driven and obsessed (in a non-crazy way) about it, and even devotes a blog to the goal. She also has a mean right hook, and if you're ever on a mechanical bull in a bar on Sunset Blvd. for the first time, she'll give you the best advice you've ever heard for staying on. I didn't listen, so I only lasted about seven seconds.

During the chat with @alliecine, I was text messaging @kimberlyprendez, and immediately told her what was going on. I used the opportunity to tell Allie why I did what I did (I pretty much told her what I told you guys earlier in the chapter), and took responsibility for it. I wasn't trying to win her back as much as I was trying to get everything out in the open so that there wasn't anything unresolved, and we could move on as friends.

Except that now she was on the fence again about dating.

I told her, as a friend, that she should do what was best for her. Then I told her, as someone who wanted her more than @jasonburns wants a lead role in a Michael Bay film, that I wanted to... well, this is exactly what I said:

robgokeemusic (12:12:52 AM): **I want to date you, and only you, and I want to see where it goes. I want to be open to the possibility that it may not end if things progress in a positive way. I want to watch movies with you all night, I want to hear you talk for hours and hours, I want to slide my hands along the side of your face, pull you close and kiss you, I want to laugh with you, I want to do mundane things like grocery shopping, because we will make it fun, I want to know that if this doesn't work I still gave it everything I had. THATS what I want.**

And she said:

allie        (12:14:51 AM): you're so unbelievably sweet and I think you've got a plan 😊

So at 1am, I jumped in my car and drove 30 miles to her apartment to kiss her pretty face for the first time.

Sorry, there's no screenshot for that.

We've had many conversations about this gap in our relationship, what I now refer to as "The Hiccup," and we've gone back and forth about what date is our actual anniversary. I decided for us during the drive back from the Tucson Film & Music Festival months later.

I was driving @brownambassador's car (he was moving his stuff to LA) behind @alliecine, and texting. Yes, while I was driving. Technically, I wasn't in California at the time, so I wasn't breaking the law. Also, I was in the desert at like 6am, and there were no other cars around. Don't ever tell people on Twitter that you're tweeting while you're driving, because they'll come unglued. It's worse than saying you're cutting up kittens. Once, I made a joke about tweeting while driving, (it was an obvious joke), something about using a laptop, tweeting, and putting on makeup at the same time. Some guy in the U.K. tweeted me back and called me an "arsehole" for tweeting and driving. I wasn't tweeting and driving, but I was annoyed by his judgmental attitude, so I came back with something about there being a big stick up his butt and that he should get it removed. He unfollowed me immediately, to which I reciprocated.
Anyway, I decided, while driving across the desert, that May 21st, our first date, was our anniversary, because, despite "The Hiccup," that was the day I started to fall in love with her.

I just didn't know it at the time.

This was the point, almost to the day, when EVERYTHING changed. There is now Rob pre-@alliecine, and Rob post-@alliecine, like the Old and New Testament. No, I'm not comparing myself to Jesus. He has enough to live up to without having to deal with MY rep. In fact, if I bumped into Jesus somewhere around town, like, @thecounter restaurant (and you know Jesus would be there because their burgers are unfrakingbelievable. I'm sure he even has his own table there, with a placard that says "Reserved For Jesus."), I'd be waving across the restaurant and yelling, "Hey, Jesus! Remember me?" And Jesus would turn away like he didn't know who I was and say, "Is that.... Oh, Jesus Christ," because he's really the only one that can get away with that. And I'd go up to the table and say "Hey, Jesus, I left you a message, why didn't you call back?" And Jesus would say, "Look, I like you, OK? But I can't be seen with you anymore. You're bringing me down with you. You need to leave before my friends get here. And put on some pants already, you're embarrassing yourself." And I would say "But you talk to @aaronkaiser, and he doesn't wear pants." Jesus would respond with, "Yeah, but he doesn't talk about his penis on Twitter like you do. People are talking." Then @jamiefishback and @aaronkaiser would show up and Jesus would pretend I wasn't there, and I'd walk away dejected, until @kevinrieplmusic called me over to his table. "He won't talk to me either. Sit down and have a beer with me." And then when Jesus leaves with his peeps, I pants @jamiefishback on his way out the door, because @aaronkaiser already isn't wearing any.

@kevinrieplmusic I smell an asshole. Its coming from... your studio. ;)

robgokee
Rob Gokee

Meanwhile, on Twitter, things were moving like a snowball downhill. My sarcastic, acerbic, pantsless tweeting was suddenly attracting all these new people I hadn't spoken to before. And not just perverts like @dailyactor, real people. Filmmaker people, which was my intention all along, but who knew that my change in "style" on Twitter was going to be helpful at wrangling them.

Some of you might not be comfortable telling your life story on Twitter; I have a lot of friends on Twitter who keep their home life separate and private. Obviously I don't have an issue with it, because I'm writing a damn book about my life, but (for me) the key to success on Twitter has been my candid and open dialogue with the people I follow and follow me. I've said this before, and I'm going to say it again.

Just be yourself.

Dating @alliecine came with certain "changes" I needed to adjust to quickly. And by quickly I mean overnight. I'm a composer. I like being isolated and introverted for days at a time, holed up and writing music. It's part of the gig. Most composers are like that. Allie is a Producer, and a Producer gets work by networking. It takes a lot of networking to land gigs, so you have to spend time constantly attending multiple events, sometimes in the same night. @alliecine is very good at this. I realized, before our first date, that if I was going to date her, I was going to need to shake off the introversion and jump in headfirst.

In June, we averaged about seven events a week, every week, for the entire month. Some of these were breakfast and lunch meetings, but a lot of them were evening networking events. Internally I was kicking and screaming at the thought of schmoozing with lots of people I didn't know, but on the outside I tried to be the guy I was on Twitter.

It was working.

The thing about networking is that, if you do it often enough, you start to see the same groups of people at different events. This is a good thing, because then you get to know them, they introduce you to their people, who might introduce you to their people... you get the picture.

The main topic of the Meetup? Twitter.
I talked about ALL of youse guys. Most
of it was good. Except for
@jamiefishback, I warned them.

11:01 PM Jul 5th 2009 from TweetDeck                    Delete

robgokee
Rob Gokee

One of the first events I went to with Allie was the
The Entrepreneur Connection (LA), a small business
meetup group run by @alaiawilliams. Alaia is a
wonderful organizer, and the event turned out to be
more beneficial than I expected it to be. As we went
around the room, I talked about my profession as a
composer (I hadn't decided to write a book at that
point) and how marketing on Twitter had benefited
both myself and @alliecine. After the meeting, I was
approached by @mischief_mari, who was a reporter
looking for people to interview for her blog. She
wanted to do an interview, video shoot and take
photographs, talking about my job and Twitter. I
was excited, it was one of those moments (I still
have them) when you realize the power of
networking, and how it really works as long as you're
willing to interact.

Which sounds suspiciously like my marketing
strategy for Twitter.

I'm here, but I'm working quietly. Even
though she's 25 miles away, I'm trying
not to wake @alliecine w/ excessive
noise. Lest I be killed.

12:45 PM Jul 15th 2009 from TweetDeck                   Delete

robgokee
Rob Gokee

117

I started to get more work, but most of it was still coming from Twitter. People were messaging me off-site and asking to meet about scoring projects. People outside of Twitter wanted to know how it worked. Another networking event I attended in June was @jamiefishback's "Tweetup," my first one.

The concept of a Tweetup is simple, it's just a networking event designed around people you know or want to get to know on Twitter. You set up an invitation online, figure out the when and where, and tweet repeatedly so that people are aware it's happening. If you're smart, you set it up so that people bring either drink or food (let them choose), like any other party. This turns it into kind of a potluck; you end up with more refreshments that you can actually consume in one night. Check out http://twtvite.com, it's a great site for organizing the event and sending out notifications by tweet.

@jamiefishback's was a BBQ, so he provided the burgers and dogs, and we (the attendees) provided everything else. Jamie held his at his own home, which means he's either very trusting or very stupid. I know Jamie, and if I had to choose I'd say "trusting" is the right answer. @alliecine and I had been together less than a week when the Tweetup happened, and had only attended one other event together, a screening of a film I scored. Jamie's Tweetup was a huge success. It was the second time I got to hang out with @cartermason, I met @aaronkaiser for the first time, I got to talk to @ginayates in person, @JonathanNail (who wasn't able to make it) brewed his own beer and provided a keg in his absence, and Ron Jeremy showed up. Yeah, you heard me. Don't ask.

118

That Tweetup was one of the first doors I opened to the group of people I network with the most now, and I met every one of them on Twitter. All I had to do was show up and be social. It was also the first time that I realized people expected me to be, in person, who I was on Twitter. I'm pretty "free" when I write, and I will usually say things that I wouldn't say in real life. That no longer applies, thanks to Twitter. I realized I liked being the outgoing person I was on Twitter instead of the introvert I had been for all of my adult (and most of my childhood) life.

There was just one problem. I didn't expect to fall in love.

# Chapter 11: July 2009
## More Changes Than I Can Shake A Pair of Pants At

I am in a VERY good mood today. It's up to all of you to try and break it. Go ahead, do your worst. Dead puppies? Don't care, I'm happy.

robgokee
Rob Cokan

Clown run over by a bus full of children? Still not changing my mood.

robgokee
Rob Cokan

That's right; I just used the famous "L Word." Not THAT one. The other one.

I'm lying slightly. I knew very well I was going to fall in love with @alliecine if I started dating her. The process was already in motion before I asked her out.

I'm very in tune with my feelings, which you already know because, if I wasn't, I wouldn't be writing this book. Or the book would be really boring, like:

*"I tweeted from the grocery store. Then I went to the bathroom and tweeted some more. Twitter is a good thing, because it helps you meet new people. The End. P.S. @cartermason made me write that he is a cool dude."*

I started dating @alliecine with the realization that a) I wasn't in this if it was going to be short term, and b) if I was going to date her, I had to be willing to open up and let her in, with the risk that I could get my heart broken again if it didn't work out.

It's always worth it (to me) to take the risk that comes with falling in love. Everyone gets their heart broken at some point in their life. If you close yourself off to future opportunities, sure, you're minimizing the risk of ever getting hurt again. But you're also missing out on all the good stuff that comes with falling in love.

S to the M to the I to the T to the T to
the E to the N. Times 1000.

3:04 PM Jul 6th, 2009 from TweetDeck          Delete

robgokee
Rob Gokee

If you ask @kimberlyprendez, I was heading down the L-shaped path before our first date.

**Me**: Hello?
Kim: Hey. I've decided I don't want you to write shit about me in the book.
**Me**: Why not?
Kim: Because you're bound to slip up and talk about how I was in jail for dog house arson, or how I never wear clothes to the supermarket, or how I used to be a man...
**Me**: Don't worry; I'd never give any of that stuff away.
Kim: Good. Why'd you call?
**Me**: I didn't. You called me. Are you still drunk? It's 9am.

Kim: No, this is a new drunk. I started at 7:30 this morning.

**Me**: Is there something you wanted? (glances at book readers) They're getting impatient.

Kim: Oh, yeah. I think you're in love with Allison.

**Me**: That's drunk talk.

Kim:

**Me**: Kim?

Kim: Sorry, I was busy throwing up in the sink. Do you think I should wash those dishes again? It rinses right off.

**Me**: I don't care; I don't eat at your house. You're wrong. I'm not in love yet.

Kim: Fine. But don't text me in the middle of the night, telling me I'm right. Not because I won't listen, because I'll be passed out from all this rum.

**Me**: Don't worry, I won't.

Later that night:

Kim: Hullllo?

**Me**: Dammit.

Kim: Toldja so. (hangs up)

All the L talk came to a head at therapy one day.

@alliecine just dissed Lost. If I didn't love her I would be SO out of here. Except there's beer & we're making fun of The Core.

robgokee
Rob Gokee

I had an epiphany. I hadn't been able to figure out what was different about dating @alliecine, but there definitely was something that made her stand out.  It took therapy (and a lot of tacos. Why tacos? Because I'm never not eating tacos.) to realize that it was her strength.  I'd never dated someone so "strong" before.  And I don't mean that in a "closed off impenetrable fortress" kind of way, but in a "know what she wants and won't stop 'til she gets it" kind of way.  I think of myself that way.

I spent a lot of time sidetracked from my goals because sometimes life takes you in a different direction for awhile, but I saw a pattern that had formed when I wasn't paying attention.

@alliecine had been the "break" in the pattern.

I'm drinking coffee from a mug that says "New Jersey" with a heart below it. Clearly I'm not in Kansas anymore. I'm in @alliecine's hood.

robgokee
Rob Gokee

## Telling Her

I knew I was going to drop the L Bomb weeks before I did it.  But I waited. I wanted it to come at the right time, and not freak her out.  So I had a conversation with one of her best friends, @ekfomo.

**Me**: Yo.
Erin: I told you to stop calling here.
**Me**: I've got a question.
Erin: You keep thinking I'm your friend, but I really don't like you.
**Me**: I want to tell Allie I love her, but I'm not sure when to do it.

Erin: I'm calling the cops on the other line and telling them that you're harassing me. I'm sure it's not the first time they've been there.
**Me**: I need some advice.
Erin: Don't say it during sex. (hangs up)

@ekfomo and I have become good friends. She can hold her own against me, occasionally bests me (but don't tell her) and she makes me laugh. Also, she likes to screengrab my Twitter feed when I talk smack about Facebook, and then post it on my Facebook wall for all to see. She's a crafty one. She's an incredible single mom who puts her kid above everything. She's also annoying and a pain in the ass.

I just left a FB update that was basically me sticking my tongue out at the Twitter-bashers on there. And my middle finger.

robgokee
Rob Gokee

I told @alliecine I was in love with her on July 5th. She didn't throw up on me, so I assumed it went well.

Harry Potter tickets bought. I'll be tweeting from the line at 830pm. If it's hot, @alliecine & I are going topless. Her car, I mean.

robgokee
Rob Gokee

I thought June was a busy month, but it didn't hold a candle to July. Holy crap. Remember all the work I didn't have in the spring because everything was on hold? It all rained down on me in July. I was working on 2 features, 2 shorts and 2 webseries all at the same time. I was juggling more balls than @bekemeyer on a Friday night in Vegas at the all-male review. It was a good kind of busy though, and of those 6 projects, 4 of them were from Twitter. It still fascinates me how much the workload was like an avalanche. I'd been yodeling at the mountain for months, and suddenly it was bearing down on me 200 mph.

I was also driving all the time. There was 40 miles between @alliecine's place and mine, and then there were meetings all over Southern California. I didn't mind. I felt more alive than I ever had in my life, and constantly being on the move was a big part of it. I found that I liked being around lots of people, I had far more fun than being cooped up at home. It also made me more appreciative of the time I did get to spend at home.

It's a good thing too, because @alliecine came built in with her own gang. Where I had just a handful of close friends I hung out with, Allie had 2 dozen of them. Within the first 2 weeks of dating her, I'd systematically met all of them. And survived. Fortunately, she spread them out instead of making me meet everyone in one lump. It was interesting to me to see the dynamic of the group, these people who had spent college together and were still hanging out regularly five plus years later. It was something I'd never experienced before, and really enjoyed being part of the "group."

A big part of the relationship required me to just "let go" and "run with it," no matter what we were doing. Although I'm impulsive, I also tend to over-think everything to the point of nausea. This was the first time in my life that I didn't over-analyze everything. I didn't think I'd like living my life this way, because I'd never done it before. It's freeing.

It also gets you a lot more work when you're social. I'd never had trouble finding work before, but being outgoing caused me to hit the motherload in the summer of '09.

@MrRaphe If you've been staring at your dog staring at the fly, you need some new hobbies. I'll come over & we'll play quarters.

robgokee
Rob Cokee

We were going to film festivals like mad; @alliecine produced a film called "Rooftop" (@rooftopmovie) that was getting into every festival under the sun. That summer, in Los Angeles alone, we went to 5 festivals that were screening the short film.

That's when I kept running into @MrRaphe, who went to school with @alliecine and is a Director of Photography and photographer. Raphe is funny, over the top, and we think alike on quite a few topics. I didn't realize it, but his photographing skilz would come in handy for something I'd had an idea for a few weeks prior, and been percolating in my busy brain.

This book.

So that you guys don't think you're missing out, I just cleaned the toilet. FYI.

robgokee
Rob Gokee

## The Book

Just before the influx of work had started, I came up with the idea for a book. If it had been a few weeks later, literally, the book wouldn't have happened because I was so busy with film scoring.

I was driving one afternoon on the freeway in LA, which is more like "parking," and I thought that it would be interesting to write a book about my marketing style on Twitter, because I spent all my time doing it. But there were already books like that on the market; I needed it to have my "stamp" on it. So I called my friend @brianspaeth for advice.

Brian is an author and filmmaker. He's written two books and produced a feature film called "Who Shot Mamba?" He also does actoring, which is similar to writering, but much different. I conference called Brian one morning on my way across town to get his opinion.

Brian: Hello?
**Me**: Hey, it's Rob.
Brian: Hold on. (holds phone away from face) How much, baby? (pauses) What do I get for that? (pauses) That's it? Never mind. Have a good day. (pauses) Sir. (rolls up window)
**Me**: You there?
Brian: Yeah, I was trying to buy, umm, oranges on the freeway offramp.

**Me**: Uh huh.

Brian: I'm a busy man. I've got writering to do, a basketeyball game to play, and a meeting with Brad Radby at 6. What can I do for you?

**Me**: I want to write a book.

Brian: About me? Cool.

**Me**: No, about me.

Brian: No one's written a book about me before. Will there be drawings?

**Me**: The book is about me, it's about my experience on Twitter.

Brian: What's a "Twitter?"

**Me**: You know, the website.

Brian: You want to write a book about my website? (turns to readers) http://www.brian23.com, new readers welcome. It's more interesting that this crap. (turns back) I thought the book was about me.

**Me**: It's about me.

Brian: That's what I said.

**Me**: (silence)

Brian: I think it's a good idea.

**Me**: Really? You think people will buy it?

Brian: As long as you don't talk about yourself. You're not going to talk about the whole "pantsless" thing are you? That'll be death for your book.

**Me**: I don't know.

Brian: I don't get that anyway. How do you function without pants?

**Me**: It's just a "thing," I'm not really always pantsless.

Brian: Whatever, man. Make sure you talk about my acting career.

**Me**: But the book is about-

Brian: And my athleticism. And my hair. You need to talk about my cool-guy haircut. I can send you pictures.

**Me**: Thanks, but-

Brian: Hey, this conversation isn't going to be in the book, is it?
**Me**: No.
Brian: Good. I've gotta go.  Good luck.

And so the book was born.  And it only took a month to write.

Del Taco drive thru. I have the best
girlfriend in the entire world. Those two
things are not related.

12 37 AM Jul 2nd, 2009 from UberTwitter                    Delete

robgokee
Rob Gokee

OK, maybe a little longer than a month.

# Chapter 12: August 2009
## The Day My Rolodex Exploded

Why am I up? Oh, yeah, the moving thing for @alliecine is today.

5:04 AM Aug 1st 2009 from UberTwitter · Delete

 robgokee
Rob Gokee

August started with moving boxes and a big white van. Allie was moving in with a new roommate. Originally I thought this was why she dated me in the first place, and expected to be dumped right after the last box was brought through the door. But she kept me after the move, so she must have some other big event that she's holding out for.

@alliecine was only moving across town, so we spent the first 2 days of August hauling stuff into a new place. That's where I met @vianessa, Allie's new roommate. @vianessa is great, but don't ever argue with her, because it doesn't matter if you're right and you have irrefutable facts to back it up, she'll wear you down to the point that you think you're wrong anyway. She's that persuasive.
And stubborn.

She's also an actress, so she's very good at "acting" like she enjoys having me around, and I buy it. If I'm ever with a producer who's casting a female role, she gets my vote, because anyone who can pretend to like me so well that I'm unaware gets a gold star. A good example of that is @axisofphilippe. He fakes it all the time. He's just not as good at it.

## Closure

The week before moving, I had coffee with the ex-girlfriend. It was... odd. The only reason we even met up was to exchange a box of her stuff that had been sitting in my closet. She needed it back; I didn't want to see it every time I opened the closet door & I was out of matches, so we arranged a meeting.

We hadn't spoken to or seen each other since the day she left the apartment, so needless to say it was a very strange experience seeing her again. We headed up the street to a nearby coffee shop and waited for a table. There was a moment, and I remember it clearly, when, in a split second, I realized that I was SO glad we weren't together. The relationship had not been healthy for either one of us, and moving on was the best thing all around. It was like looking into another life, one I wasn't a part of anymore, and I had no desire to go back. And then all I could think of was getting back to @alliecine. But I was already there so I thought, "What the fuck, let's chat and pretend we both want to be there, when really we wish we were ANYWHERE else. Like at the DMV during the summer, and the air conditioning is out, and you're sandwiched between two people who haven't showered in days with a little piece of paper that says you're number 659, and they just called number 2." That place, I'd rather be there than sitting in a shitty coffee shop in Echo Park across the table from the person I didn't feel like I knew anymore.

We made small talk about family and television. Then she told me she was moving halfway across the country. You know, to the place where the guy she met on Twitter lived? Yeah, that guy. I did NOT see it coming.

At first I wanted to laugh, because it was such a huge shock that it was laughable. Like when you see one of @jfuzell's snakes eat a mouse. It's sad, but in a funny way. Not a "haha, hey, where's your kitten, and what's that other huge lump in the snake?" kind of funny, but close. I was shocked that she was making such a huge move so soon. Honestly, I really didn't care, I was just surprised. I wished her well, gave her the box, and closed the door on that chapter of my life.

Then this strange thing happened over the next 24 hours.

I got really, really pissed off.

I think it's time I go bully all the FB people for a few minutes. I have to use little words when I type over there, they're a little slow.

9 PM Aug 25th, 2009 from TweetDeck          Delete

robgokee
Rob Gokee

It was strange. I had trouble sleeping the night after the coffee meeting, and then the next day I was in the OC all day, and felt myself getting angrier and angrier. And it was affecting my tweeting, in that I dropped the F-bomb three tweets in a row.

I don't have a problem with curse words. I think there are times when they're appropriate, as long as they're not overused. My mom would say that curse words are never appropriate, but she'll also tell you I do what I want and don't follow the rules. That's why I love her. My dad has less of an issue with curse words, unless you ask him when my mom's around. I get my work ethic from my dad; he also doesn't know the meaning of "stop." Any detail-oriented tendencies I have I get from my mom. I can be anal about details, and I like dealing with numbers, and those are very much her traits.

Anyway... bad mood.

It was one of the angriest moods I've ever been in, and I had no idea why, which made me angrier. I was in Costa Mesa, and @alliecine, who saw my tweets, called me and told me to meet her in Venice at the bar where she had just finished a meeting with @cartermason and her partner Jillian (@jillyleigh). Yeah, Carter had a meeting at a bar. I know, I was shocked, too.

Jillian is also known as @NewCityJillian, she's partnered with Allie (@NewCityAllison) in her other company New City Entertainment. They help companies with social media marketing and strategy, and run seminars for parents, teaching them about social media so they know what their kids are doing online. I'm glad they weren't around when I was a kid, because they're damn good, and my parents would have been blocking sites all over the place.

I drove like 90mph from Costa Mesa to Venice, which is about a 50 mile trip. Allie had talked me into meeting them, but part of me wanted to go home and drink an entire bottle of wine while watching House in bed.

WITH Pants. That's how upset I was.

But I knew I'd feel worse if I was alone, so I opted for @alliecine, @cartermason, @jillyleigh and the bar. When I got to Venice, I had to circle the block a few times to find a parking space, and Allie jumped in the car with me to find out what was wrong. I was arguably the angriest I'd ever been.

In 10 minutes she diffused me.

With words.

I realized that I was angry about the way my relationship had ended, I was angry that I had confirmation that she had cheated, angry that there was really no warning, angry that 4 and a half years of friendship were gone in less than 30 days. It's not that I wanted any of that stuff back, I was very happy with the direction my life had taken, but I don't think I'd ever allowed myself to be angry, with the brief exception of Moving Day back in March.

3 months ago today, I took @alliecine out for our first date.

robgokee
Rob Gokee

10 minutes. That's all it took Allie to make things better. She's the best listener in the world. But I'm not going to get all gushy and gross you out. I already did that in the acknowledgments.

## Film Stuff

Boys and girls, this voyage is officially WRAPPED.

8:17 PM Aug 8th, 2009 from Uber Twitter                    Delete

robgokee
Rob Gokee

"11:11" finally wrapped this month. There had been some internal drama surrounding the project that delayed production for a few months, but Rocky weathered all of it to get to the last day of shooting. I once again tweeted from the set, except this time Rocky didn't want me giving anything away, and he really wasn't too keen on me tweeting this time around because he was trying to keep the shoot a secret. Now, I'd been tweeting from the beginning, and I thought the people following me deserved to see it through to the end. But I wanted to respect his wishes, so what could I do?

Then it hit me. Pirates.

I had this brilliant idea of "disguising" the tweets within a story, a story of a boat on a journey across the ocean that's attacked by pirates. And for all intents and purposes, it worked. Everyone got a cool pirate nickname. Although I'm sure some of my followers, especially if they jumped into the middle of the story, wondered what drugs I was taking and if someone had called health services to report me yet.

My point here is that, if you have some fun and use your imagination when you're tweeting, people will gravitate toward the funny and follow you, talk to you, maybe work with you.

I'd been part of the film since before the script was finished, so it was nice to finally see it through. Rocky had allowed me to be a part of the production side of the film, and we were officially into post.

On a side note, we were short a few extras and I was recruited to play a drug buyer.  I was happy to help out, and it fulfilled my lifelong dream.

Not of acting, of buying drugs.

**Party Time**

At the tweetup. Why aren't you here?

robgokee
Rob Gokee

In the month of August, @alliecine and I hosted not one, but TWO Tweetups of our own.  Now, I've never organized a party in my life.  In fact, I don't think I've ever had enough friends at one time to actually have a "party," but there I was, setting up two of them.

The first one was on a whim.  Allie and I took a rare day off and wanted to get away from everything.  So we decided, since summer was coming to a close and we hadn't been to the beach at all, that we were going to Zuma (in Malibu) for the day. It quickly turned into "Hey, should we invite people to join us?" The thought of turning it into a party sounded fun, so we made an impromptu announcement on Twitter that everyone within driving distance was invited.

It was a decent turnout for being last minute, about a dozen people showed up, including the fan-favorite @cartermason. Really, if you're on Twitter and not following him by now, stop reading and go look him up. If you're also a Kansas City Chiefs fan, he might kiss you on the mouth. Make him wear a condom on his tongue, though, that thing has been places I've only heard about it stories.

The Zuma Tweetup was Sunday. On Tuesday, we noticed a plea on Twitter from @jazmoore, who had traveled to LA from upstate New York. She'd been in Los Angeles a week and hadn't met one Twitter person yet, and her trip was coming to a close. So @alliecine and I took it upon ourselves to have a Tweetup for her, so she could try and catch all of us at once. Because we had a little more lead time, and it was a bit more central in location (Allie's apartment complex is more "centered" in LA, and she had a pool & BBQ area), we had a great turnout for Jaz's maiden voyage to SoCal. 20-30 showed up; @jazmoore entertained everyone by wearing a cake on her head and singing lewd limericks while swinging an empty bottle of wine.

Tweetups are a great way to meet people on Twitter that you're interested in working with because, unlike the creepy weirdos in chat-rooms back in the 90's (I think back then @JonathanNail used to pretend he was a 90 year old producer so he could pick up on 20 year old starlets), Twitter users are all
138

about networking, and making things happen. It's the thing (in my opinion) that separates it from MySpace, Facebook, and the hordes of other social media networks that I belong to and don't bother posting on.

Twitter people make things happen.

http://twitpic.com/fras5 - La super-rica taqueria in Santa Barbara with @alliecine. This was just her order. Beer not pictured.

robgokee
Rob Gokee

Allie and I also took our first trip away together in August. We drove up to San Luis Obispo (stopping at one of the best taco places I've ever eaten at, La Super-Rica in Santa Barbara. There's always a line, but it's worth it, trust me), Avila Beach and stopped by the wineries on the way back. It was a wonderful trip, and I tweeted lots of pictures.

That's right; you can post pictures on Twitter. Most smartphone Twitter applications allow you to use the camera attached to your phone to take and upload pics using services like TwitPic. It's just another way to chronicle your life and share things with the rest of your followers. But don't take pictures of your butt and post them. I lost 45 followers that day.

It was my first time wine tasting, I loved it so much I wanted to erect a tent at Baileyana Winery and live there. We spent one morning on Avila Beach, where I bought new sunglasses only to have them stolen by the ocean, which prompted buying another pair of sunglasses.

It was nice to get away from everything, and it was nice to be there with Allison. I think I even left my laptop at home. If you know me you know that this is more disconnected than I ever get.

Oh, I tweeted. I always tweet.

It's become normal for me to tweet from everywhere about everything. There are obviously some things I keep private, and do, lest the wrath of @alliecine comes down upon me, but I try and be as open as I can be on Twitter. You book readers know by now that I've said things here I don't even say on Twitter.

Aren't YOU guys special.

We're getting close to the end, this is the 11th month. Trust me, September was even busier than August. Don't worry, I'm not done yet.

Or, depending on what you think:

I'm sorry, I'm still not done.

# Chapter Thirteen: September 2009
## Running Down the Path Pantsless

I am officially tweeting with no pants
right now. It helps with the writing
process.

robgokee
Rob Gokee

The trend of work continued into September; it was getting a little insane. I also had a book to write, and people were already asking me about when it was going to be done. Sleep is something I've wished so many times I could forgo. I know how important it is, I just need the time for other things.

Things like the start of production for "SOLO the Series" (@SOLOtheSeries).

This was the first project @alliecine and I were working on together, and it got underway in September. Creator @JonathanNail pulled out all the stops, and even built a spaceship in his garage to shoot it. Yes, my job is not like your job.
I actually helped on set for SOLO, I worked the catering table, gripped, and even gaffed once (it's a job that involves going up and down a ladder about 600 times to make minor adjustments, then you move it all to another spot after 15 minutes of

shooting.  Right after you beat the Director of Photography with an aluminum bat for 10 minutes. It's actually a lot like being a composer, except I get to sit in a comfy chair in one place while I make 600 changes.  There's a big difference, trust me.)

I lost 1 follower in the last hour. I really, really hope it's because I used the word PENIS in a tweet. #Penis

12:54 PM Sep 15th, 2009 from web                    Delete

robgokee
Rob Gokee

I took more meetings with people I met on Twitter.  @HeathVinyard and I met about scoring his webseries "End Result" (@EndResultSeries) over tacos; his passion and excitement reminded me of my first meeting with @JonathanNail.

I started working on the webseries (do you see a pattern here? Webseries are the new "thing") "Fallen" (@FallenSeries) with E.E. Charlton-Trujillo.
Fallen is very *Buffy*-like in its cinematography and story, so it's an understatement to say that I was excited.

On top of that, I was scoring the trailer for "11:11," the feature film "K-Town" and the short films "Thank You Mr. Patterson" (Directed by @Sabra14) and "Taking The Fall."
One thing I've learned as a composer for film and television over the last five years is that it's always feast or famine.  You have these times (like the spring of 2009) when there's nothing going on.  And then it's like all the directors you're attached to met up at some secret location, like a Denny's in The

Valley, and timed all their films to hit post at the same time just to drive you crazy. It's really not as terrible as I let on, and I prefer to work this way. You just adapt your work methods and schedule to accommodate this kind of insanity. The other option is to find another career, because it's always going to be like that. I love it. I love the rush of having a short deadline and forcing yourself to come up with ideas. I love being so busy you can't think straight. I love staying up til 3am and getting up at 7am, excited to start all over again. It's the best time I've ever had in my life, and the best job I've ever had, or could ever ask for.

Good morning tweeple! Hmmm what to do today.

8:01 AM Sep 5th, 2009 from Echofon      Reply  Retweet

kevinrieplmusic

@kevinrieplmusic Find a personality?

8:05 AM Sep 5th, 2009 from TweetDeck in reply to kevinrieplmusic      Delete

robgokee
Rob Gokee

I took a trip with @alliecine to the Tucson Film and Music Festival to see @michaelskvarla and @alliecine's film "Junkyard" play at the fest. @alliecine went to the University of Arizona in Tucson, so she took the opportunity to show me around her old stomping grounds. It was a great five day trip; I got to hang out with @brownambassador, who is not only an amazing DP and director, but a great friend. He went to college with @alliecine, and is like the brother I never had. He also has very busy hands that always seem to find their way into my pants. I make weird, sexual comments about Jorge not because I'm gay, but because it makes Allie squirm.

This month I also started managing multiple Twitter accounts, because I created one for the book, @FailWhaleBook.

I chose to create a separate Twitter account for The Book (this was how I referred to it before I had a title) because I wanted a place that was just about promoting the book. Most of the time. I broke that rule a few times when I tweeted The Book account like it was a horny teenager, hitting on all my followers (both sexes) and having it hook up with @NewCityAllison. The point is that I wanted some separation between the two accounts, one of which I was tweeting as a composer and not made of paper and glue.

Third-party applications for Twitter let you manage as many Twitter accounts as you need (@alliecine has almost 12, one for each film she's producing. Yeah, she's a fucking machine.).

There are plenty of great programs out there to use with Twitter, but I am in love with TweetDeck. They're not paying me to rave about them, they may even ask me to remove this after they've seen the cover, but this is an unsolicited endorsement. The interface is so easy to use, there are multiple ways to set up your tweets so that you don't miss anything, and running multiple accounts is a breeze. Once you've set up your Twitter account and have gotten the hang of the basics, I suggest you download TweetDeck and give it a spin.

And if you're not on Twitter by the time you reach this sentence in the book... what are you waiting for?

Jump in.

# Chapter 14
## Yes, I'm Finally Shutting Up

We've reached the end of this tale.

Not MY tale, that's still happening.

My first year on Twitter ends in September of 2009, and I'm writing this epilogue in January of 2010. I suppose you might be wondering what other crap I've gotten myself into so far, which is now referred to as Year Two of My Life On Twitter. Perhaps I should catch you up on the goings on of the people in my life.

@cartermason is now a rodeo clown in Colorado. He's been in and out of the hospital with his arms broken four times each, his legs three times in three different places, and his pelvis is now made of steel, but he gets all the rum he can drink as payment, so he's happy.

@jamiefishback is now a senator in Wisconsin. He just weathered a scandal based around his fondness for sheep, which is related to a bizarre pregnancy that even I can't talk about here.

@ekfomo got rich inventing a combination vibrator/hand mixer, but lost it all when she was sued by an irate housewife who was injured. She now lives on a small island in the South Pacific with a harem of tanned men who wait on her hand and foot.

@jillyleigh married a movie star whose name I can't divulge here, and went on to live in Brentwood with him, birthing 6 children while running her own corporation that manufactures a special kind of programmable paper clip that talks to you and tells you what you're clipping together.

@JonathanNail became the first man on Mars, which has always been his dream. Unfortunately, the trip drove him mad and he disabled the navigation on the shuttle during his return trip. He's still orbiting Saturn. Upside down.

@brianspaeth parlayed his movie career into a professional hockey contract, but he was tragically killed when a fan threw a copy of his book at him during a game, and it caused him to fall on the ice and break his neck. That fan was @laurierecords.

As for @alliecine and I, we got rich manufacturing our own moonshine out of corn syrup and rubbing alcohol, so we moved to a farm in Kansas. We're pregnant with kid number eight; @betenich and @jfuzell live with us, and have a herd of cats. FYI, a "herd" of cats is 244 of them. They're kind of hard to round up; we've found that the elephant we bought works really well at keeping them from getting out of hand. I gave up composing music to raise cattle while Allie crotchets cloth napkins and sells them online.

## What's REALLY Been Happening

Seriously, things are (if you can believe it) even busier, and things with @alliecine are going great. We had Thanksgiving at my house, with 10 friends and family, something I've never done. We held another Tweetup here, too, Champagne and Cookies, and had a great turnout. I even got a new gig scoring a webseries from someone I met at the Tweetup.

We spent the holidays in New Jersey with Allie's family, and I survived. I saw Manhattan for the first time in my life, and fell in love with it. We both have so much going on the first quarter this year I might actually implode, but I'm loving every minute of it.

Allison is the love of my life, and she is the catalyst of the largest change that's ever occurred in my existence. She is my best friend, and she shows me every day, multiple times, how much she loves me back. I don't know what the future holds, I've learned not to try and predict it, but no matter what happens from this day forward, the events that occurred on 2008-09 on Twitter and in my life will always be integral to what happens in my future.

149

I'd like to thank all of you for reading this book. My hope is that I've been able to teach you something about Twitter, and entertain you in the process.

The people that make up my Twitter stream are important to me, because I consider them friends. Not only as a business person, but on a personal level I care about what's going on in their lives, and they care and take part in mine. That's the most important thing, and my favorite part about Twitter.

Listening to You.